BEING IN ALL RESPECTS READY FOR SEA

Herbert Gordon Male, Sub Lieut., pictured in June 1943.

BEING IN ALL RESPECTS READY FOR SEA

Herbert Gordon Male

JANUS PUBLISHING COMPANY
London, England

First published in Great Britain 1992 by
Janus Publishing Company

© Herbert Gordon Male 1992

British Library Cataloguing in Publication Data

Male, Herbert, *1916–*
   Being in all respects ready for sea.
   I. Title
   359.34092

   ISBN 1 85756 030 2

Cover design David Murphy

Phototypeset by Intype, London

Printed and bound England by
Antony Rowe Ltd, Chippenham, Wiltshire

Dedicated to Albert Watson, coxswain of HMS *Syringa*, without whose example, guidance and unstinting help I would never have sat my leading seaman's examination.

Also to the few who survived the sinking of HMS *Cocker* and to the memory of the many who did not.

'You come of a breed of men the very wind of whose name has swept the ultimate seas'

J. M. Barrie

Contents

My Choice of This Title

During these wartime experiences in the Royal Navy, I was always fascinated by the couching of the signal that sent us back to sea.

The sequence of events that evoked this signal were always the same.

The first and most immediate responsibility of all officers in command of HM ships, upon coming in from sea, was to bring their ships back to that state of readiness that enabled them to return to sea.

This entailed refuelling and re-storing ship and attending to any defects. As soon as these were accomplished, a signal to that effect was sent to base.

Upon receipt of this signal, base would inform the originator that she was now considered to be at a required number of hours 'notice' and only if this state was four hours or more could leave be granted.

A subsequent signal would arrive putting the ship under 'Immediate notice.'

From here it was only a matter of time before the familiar and time-honoured 'Being in all respects ready for sea, you will slip and proceed,' etc, signal arrived.

Thus, the sea-worthiness of each HM ship was the sole responsibility of its commanding officer.

Introduction

As a quarry boy of fourteen years of age, and on into manhood, I had enjoyed an independence of spirit shared by few of the working class. As boys we ran free, and in the old quarries built cabins of stone, where we ate potatoes stolen from the nearby allotments, half-cooked and with blackened skins. We bathed and fished among the rocks we knew so well and in the long summer holidays camped, picked blackberries, cooked limpets, ate sour apples and kept secret the birds' nests that we knew.

As a prelude to our joining our fathers in the quarries, we carried in a 'go cart' quarry tools to be sharpened by the blacksmith, working in our dinner-hour or after school. Later, we learnt that the arduous work in the quarries, the wind, the rain, cold hands and feet, were all to become *the* winter-time lot of the outdoor pieceworker.

They were bitter days, spent with chapped hands, trying to beat a fast-rising tide at Castletown pier, learning all the time how to handle the mooring ropes and wires, getting to know my way around the coasters and sailing barges that took our stone to London, Belfast and Glasgow.

Around me all the time, in this hard manual work, was the Royal Navy.

As we worked picket boats from all the great names among warships came flurrying, with their human cargoes, in to the pier where we worked, names like HMS *Warspite* (how I thrilled some years later to watch her bombard the German defences on the Normandy coast); HMS *Barham* – I saw her blow up and sink, with grievous loss of life, in the Mediterranean; the *Nelson* and the *Rodney*, the big cruisers; and who could forget the 'Mighty Hood'?

Entire ships' companies were regularly marched around the Island's roads, headed by a Royal Marine band: all very stirring stuff for an impressionable boy.

Throughout the whole of this period, how lucky I had been to have been taught my skills – I only realised this in later years –

by men of great integrity, who held the 'work ethic' high among their puritan principles.

The study of the rock formations and strata that form the beds of the Portland Stone, how to make use of these natural beds and joints, how best to release these great rocks from where they had lain for a hundred and fifty million years: absorbing all this knowledge meant the difference between good and poor earnings, intelligent men and those who were content with just beer and skittles.

How many times, as a boy, had I been told, 'If you can work and talk, then stop talking, and work a bit harder.'

The awesome power of the sea, never far away from us on our tiny island, pounding on the rocky coast or sucking on the violent Chiswel Beach – the ebb and flow of the tides that go to make the dreaded Portland Race. In thick fog, the 'mooing' of the long-gone 'Shambles' lightship', guarding its treacherous shifting sands. Seagulls diving and gliding against the full south-west gale, driving rain, or flat-a-calm with the sun rising out of the sea.

The great liners, and their lesser brothers, tramping home from the seas of the world, calling in for their 'up'-Channel pilots.

The first of the new design 'Tribal'-class destroyers doing their speed and working-up trials, the annual assembly of the Home and Mediterranean Fleets in the harbour – all these sights and sounds had been part of my upbringing.

I make no attempt to apologise for writing this in the first person, for how else could these experiences and stories, of so formative a part of my life, have been written?

Neither do I claim any literary skills, for at no time did I sit down with the intention of writing a book; this is no more than, in my retirement, committing some of my experiences to paper and then threading them all together.

Foreword

My first meeting with Bertie Male was in the gymnasium of HMS *Lochailort*, in the wilds of Scotland, where selected naval ratings were to be trained as prospective officers. We had all donned white cap-bands in place of the normal blue ones and had become known as 'cadet ratings'.

The spartan life that we were expected to lead in landing craft and the coming invasion demanded, it was thought, physical as well as mental fitness.

In charge of our physical training was a quite ferocious PTI (Physical Training Instructor), who became known as 'Peniteniary Pete', because, it was learnt, he had been doing a similar job at the Royal Naval Detention Quarters. In his training manual, stamped on every page, were, we imagined, the words 'Scowls will be worn at all times.'

'Up the rope you go,' he snarled . . . each rating grabbing his rope, and tried to climb up, but hung like a sack of potatoes at the bottom . . . all except Bertie Male, who shinnied up like a monkey, touched the ceiling and climbed down again.

'You're all sloppy, slow and out of condition,' snarled Pete. 'But before you leave here, I'll have each one of you climbing your rope without using your feet . . . I'll see to that. Only one of you is in proper condition.'

Amazingly, those of us who survived the course were in fact able to do just that, so fit had we all become.

It was February, the Scottish winter was bitter and in unheated Nissan huts we studied navigation, seamanship, boat-handling, pilotage, signals, meteorology, tides, charts, aircraft recognition, power of command, gunnery, the general duties of an officer and a thousand other naval matters. On the parade-ground, we fell in endlessly, drilled, marched, did ceremonial rifle drill and PT until we groaned.

On the loch itself we put theory into practice, with boat-handling, rowing, sailing and taking command of our crews as officers of the watch.

We learned also the various marks of respect for senior officers and a multitude of naval customs and traditions. The manner of our dress was under constant inspection and our 'officer-like qualities' were constantly assessed. We swam, although it was February, and practised the rescue of survivors from open boats.

There was no let-up, from dawn to dark these activities continued . . . Finally we threw ourselves into our bunks exhausted, to sleep like the dead, until at 6 a.m. we were rudely awoken by the duty PO bashing at the corrugated sheeting of the hut with a heavy cudgel, with the time-honoured 'Wakey Wakey . . . rise and shine!'

Each succeeding week seemed to produce a more rigorous physical demand, accompanied by a greater mental effort to keep abreast of our studies.

The final degradation was the end-of-course Boxing Match: each cadet was matched, weight by weight, and was expected to slog it out to the bitter end . . . We were told, 'The Commander likes to see plenty of blood and guts, it's better to be a blood-splattered loser than a clean winner . . . however much you get knocked about, you must keep coming back for more . . . even if you have to come back on your knees.'

At long last the course was over and those who had survived (about half the original number) were invited to tea with the staff in the castle where they lived.

Scowls were now replaced with smiles . . . thus did we learn that we were now commissioned sub-lieutenants in the RNVR.

Many more months of hard training were to follow, all of which led up to the D-day landings. then at 'D plus 19' came the Great Gale.

This was a totally unexpected gale of savage proportions which came out of the south-east and caused great havoc among the landing craft, with many casualties among the destroyers and other attendant ships. It badly delayed the 'build-up' and those who were caught on the 'Far Shore', as the French coast was called, had a very rough time of it. It was amid this chaos that Bertie Male distinguished himself by guiding his craft (his CO had, through inexperience, given up); it was mainly this feat which brought about his promotion to full lieutenant, with command of an American landing craft infantry (large). Thus began Bertie's voyage to the Far East.

Bertie Male was the strongest, fittest and best natural seaman I ever met in my naval career. For a while during our early training we shared a cabin and I got to know him well . . . I much admired him, then and afterwards, and am proud to account him as the best friend of my naval days and am sure that these vivid writings of his war in small ships will be a great success.

Paul Lund

P. R. Lund is the co-author of *P.Q.17: Convoy to Hell; Trawlers go to War; War of the Landing Craft; Out Sweeps; Hit the Beach; Nightmare Convoy,* etc.

Preface

Although the author and I were born on the Island, enjoyed the same free environment as children, and were later both employed in the stone industry, it was not until the war years (1939–46) that our paths crossed, he as the officer in charge of a landing craft and I as the coxswain of a fire-boat at Castletown Portland. But it was not until we had both retired that the time and the opportunity arose to get to know each other better.

Our mutual concern for everything Portland and its environs became the basis of a greater understanding between us, and it was not until then that he could bring himself to show me a manuscript that he had written years before, because he felt that the reader might think him boastful or immodest.

Nothing could be further from the truth; it is a simple yet factual account of one man's war, with all the drama, frustration and humour that that entails, and if occasionally I do detect a hint of pride in some particular relationship or happening, no wonder – there is so much to be proud of.

C. A. Durston
(*Skylark*)

As a young man, Gordon Male and I, with many others of our age, swam in the rough seas off Portland. I know of his well-respected family, possibly puritan by today's standards, whereby his sisters would have been given the uttermost privacy in the course of their young lives; so that when directed by the Admiralty to serve aboard a deep-sea trawler with hardened fishermen whose ways of living were completely foreign to that young man he was – to coin a phrase – 'like a lamb to the slaughter'.

However, having read this account of his life at sea during the 1939–45 war, I find it at least comparable to those of fellow contemporary writers, some of whom he served with.

George Davey

When I Was a Boy

When I was a boy this was home
Never far from the staring stone
Never far from the sight of sail
Ancient song of the South West gale

The salted clifftops airy wine
The freedom of the fields was mine
All children wandered free of fear
For no-one was a stranger here

The quarried lanes that ran between
Old rubble banks with scraps of green
The hunting ground of any child
Who sought the flowers rare and wild

The games we played are gone for good
That satisfied our childhood
The iron hoops we bowled along
Clay marbles with the cocks are gone

No ducky stones or whip the tin
Stone cabins with the fire of Shin
No shout of Jack, Jack shine the light
Or challenge met with stones to fight

In winter walls with music rang
The organ and the Fiddle sang
And where the new estates are now
The sound of horses under plough

No age escapes the whims of fate
But here was much to compensate
Each season brought its special joy
This was home when I was a boy

When skylarks cease to charm the skies
Or seabirds woo a rocky shore
When freedom as we know it dies
This will for me be home no more.

By kind permission of C. A. Durston
(*Skylark*)

Chapter One

From Quarry to Quay

My entry into this world was staged at No. 17 Wakeham Easton, Portland, in the July of 1916. Being the first boy grandchild, after quite a few of the other sex, my grandmother, whenever she entered the house, would ask, 'Where's the boy'? and so from that day to this I answer more readily to the name of 'Boy' than to the more formal Herbert Gordon Francis.

My grandfather on Mother's side was a master tailor in the Royal West Yorkshire Regiment, while grandmother was of the Portland family of Skinners. When the regiment was moved to Dublin, like all servicemen's wives she went with her husband; here grandfather died, leaving her to struggle back to Portland with four children. A widow's life with four children in those times must have been very difficult, but later she married a local man by the name of Pearce, who, as a widower, already had five children.

Their union was blessed with a further child and so in order to differentiate between them they used to say 'mine', 'thine' and 'ourn'.

Grandfather on my father's side was a seafaring man who probably came to the Island from Jersey. He married a Portland girl of the Hounsell family and they had eleven children, the first nine of whom were boys, so one way or another I am a bit of a mongrel.

One of my mother's favourite stories was that, when I was only three years old, I was standing on the doorstep of No. 17 with my elder sister, who was waiting for her schoolteacher, Miss Gladys Otter, to collect her to take her on to school. Upon her arrival I began to cry to go to school with my sister, so, despite my tender years, Miss Otter took me with her.

This was, of course, the Methodist school in Easton Square, where our playground was the road in front of the school. We had no school dinners or free milk in those days and most of our teachers dispensed their justice with the aid of a long cane.

I suppose we had a sort of uniform, one brought about solely by the lack of selection in boy's clothes, most of us wore a grey jersey, long-sleeved with a collar that buttoned up to the neck, longish short trousers, with woollen socks up to the knees.

The great 'Nemo' Edwards became my headmaster, with a quite formidable Miss Jeans as his assistant. Later Mr Arthur King took over and shortly after this we moved up to the New School in 1926.

This was the year of the miners' strike which became the great National Strike, but for me the more memorable, for my immature years, was the fact that we moved from Wakeham to go and live in Moorfield Road.

Here we had gas lighting instead of the old oil-lamps and shortly after this we had the new-fangled electricity installed. The one-valve crystal set came with us from Wakeham and I still remember the great thrill of all the family sitting around the table hoping to 'find' the 2LO station and the wonder of music coming to us through the airwaves.

Mr Martindale was our headmaster at the new school junior department, where I spent just over a year with Mr Bert Flann as my teacher.

Then on 'up' into the senior school, where Mr Baker, Mr Tann,

Mr Jenkins and a Miss Grey, with others completed my formal education.

Four days after my fourteenth birthday I left school – I couldn't get away fast enough, as my academic attainment had been minimal. 'Tries hard and is very willing, arithmetic weak' was one of my better end-of-term reports.

I had, however, played football for the first eleven and have a much-valued photograph to prove it, but upon reflection they were very short of left-footed players that year and as I could kick with my left foot I managed a place on the left wing.

But now I was free to follow my father into the tough outdoor life of a quarryman. Being born on the Island, we had very little other choice; son tended to follow father because we were a captive workforce. Brawn and muscle were all the masters needed in the quarries, plus no small amount of commonsense. The going was rough and the accident rate high, but at fourteen years of age who thought of anything but the freedom from school that this offered?

I was very small for my age and many doubted if I could stand the arduous life of a pieceworker. On my first morning, walking on to work with my father, a well-known ancient wit suggested that, 'It was a shame to take the poor little bugger away from his mother.'

Living on this tiny island, I have never been far away from the sea or the Navy and in those days we could collect in the harbour a vast array of warships; it was commonplace to see perhaps a dozen great battleships with attendant cruisers and destroyers lying off Castletown pier; and often, for exercise, whole ships' companies would be marched around the Island, headed by the band of the Royal Marines.

On Sunday evenings it was fashionable for whole families to walk to the common land above the naval cemetery, where, with the panorama of the Fleet lying there before them, the locals could watch and listen to the ceremony of 'Sunset' being carried out by the Royal Marines on the quarterdeck of each of the great battleships.

I had interested myself in all things naval and, to complement this, the gang of men that I had gone to work with was one of two who merged together to form a gang of eight men for the purpose of loading block Portland stone from Castletown pier into a variety of both sailing and steam ships.

These loading operations were an art in themselves and our special gang was maintained for this arduous task. It would have been easy to have had an accident, to knock a hole through the side of the ship, or to maim a fellow worker; the laws of demurrage, being what they were, demanded that work be carried out in even the most severe weather, daylight or dark. Because of these factors very long working days were quite usual: almost without knowing it, I was soaking up all matters concerning ships and the sea, so that when war came it seemed quite natural that the only place to serve was in the Navy.

I went confidently along to the recruiting office at the old Sydney Hall in Weymouth, only to be told (and this situation continued for almost eighteen months after the war had started) that the only way I could get into the Navy was to sign on for seven years in the Fleet, with an added five years in the reserve. This rather shattered me as, although the Navy was my first choice, seven years was somewhat longer than I had in mind; after all, we all thought that the war would be over by Christmas.

I need not have worried, as I finally notched up just over six years anyway. However, an understanding old chief petty officer, seeing my disappointment whispered in my ear, 'Why not go along to the Custom-House on North Quay – there they are offering "Hostilities Only" terms, but you will sign on in minesweepers.'

I signed on and in only a matter of days my papers came to report to Chatham. I had time enough to say goodbye to all my workmates and to listen to all the advice given me by those who had served in the First World War.

Chapter Two

The *Andrew*

Carrying with me, as instructed, an empty suitcase in which to
return my 'civvy' clothes, I found myself on a train bound for
Waterloo, thence onwards to Chatham. At Chatham a large chalked notice-board directed me to a corner of the platform, where
I found about twenty chaps similar to myself, all with empty
suitcases.

Holding court over all was an old stoker petty officer, who from
his looks could have been seventy years old. With almost old-
world courtesy, he *suggested* that we should all go off and get a
cup of tea as he had to wait for further arrivals. This we gladly
did and half an hour later he appeared at the doorway and told
us if we had finished to make our way along to the bus for onward
passage to Chatham barracks.

In just a short drive through the streets of Chatham, it was not hard to decide that, if our stay in this town was going to be a long one, it was going to be a very dull war.

Pulling in to the main gate we were told to dismount – and it was then that it hit us. In the twinkling of an eye our benign and of late courteous stoker PO changed into a snarling, spitting wildcat. 'Get fell in – in threes', 'Stand to attention', 'Look to your front', and 'Stand still. You've just joined the Royal Navy and this is Chatham Barracks'.

We were marched right across the vast parade-ground, in what our PO described as 'one bloody great heap', and into a large empty building, where we just stood and stood for what seemed an hour – even our PO vanished.

At last a thunderous voice bellowed out, 'What the hell are you lot doing there?' We all tried in unison to explain – but that was fatal, for we had not yet learnt that, however large or small an assembled party may be, 'someone' has to be in charge.

'Right,' said the thunderous voice, 'one of you collect your papers and bring them to me.' But our papers had already been collected by the vanished PO and so peace reigned again for another half-hour – but with much to-ing and fro-ing at the far end. Finally, each of us was supplied with a blanket and a patch on the floor on which to sleep and we were told to 'turn in and pipe down'.

One disgusted clown mumbled, 'If this is the Navy I wish I'd joined the Wrens.' It was at Chatham that a typical matelot's story was doing the rounds: 'Jack had been granted all-night leave and, to enjoy it to the full, he had booked a bed in "Aggie Weston's". Next morning, before his divisional officer, he was charged with ". . . having fallen asleep while smoking and caught his bedding alight . . ." In reply to, ". . . What have you got to say?" without the flicker of an eye, he said, "It's a lie, sir, the bed was afire when I got in." '

We spent a most uncomfortable night trying to sleep on a hard floor. Little did we know that this was to be the first of many such nights in various parts of the world.

The most enlightening experience of all was when, in what the Navy chooses to call the 'ablutions block' here, early next morning seven of us all tried to shave from one mirror!'

We will pass lightly over the first breakfast in the 'Andrew' – not a meal to be remembered: but then not even the best of chefs can do very much with cold 'herrings in tomato sauce' – hereafter known throughout the Navy as 'Errings in'. Some hours later, having marched hither and yon, it was decided that we should never have darkened Chatham's door – Lowestoft was where we rightly belonged. This being established, a great urgency took over. We were hustled like lepers to the main gate and before we understood what was going on, we were entrained to Lowestoft via London.

Having not yet been kitted out, we had yet to understand the pride that this event would for ever establish in us; later still, we would take that pride with us from ship to ship, however small, but at this moment we were not impressed. Twelve months later, when I returned to Chatham as a leading seaman to do a short gunnery course, the Navy had shaped me into accepting the fact that there is always a reason and a way of doing everything in the service.

The base at Lowestoft was, or had been before it had been commandeered by the Navy, a rather lovely seaside gardens, known as 'The Sparrows Nest', a pleasure-ground with a large concert hall and many ancillary buildings. Then the Navy descended, with its raucous bugles and 'tannoy' systems. Many thousands of raw recruits were to be documented here before the war ended and under the command of Commodore Daniel De Pass it was to become as 'pusser' (naval) a base as any of its bigger brothers. Right now it was a shambles!'

There were no barracks as such in Lowestoft; each man was billeted with civilian landladies. Some of the houses had as many as seven or more sailors and, as the base was at the Northern end of a very long seafront, many men billeted over the swing bridge at the southern end of town found that they had a good two miles to walk to the base – then back for dinner, as the Navy still called lunch, returning again for the afternoon session and then back 'home' again in the evening.

This was some eight miles per day, plus the endless square-bashing that might occur during the day's training.

If nothing else, after a spell at Lowestoft men left for sea much fitter than they had arrived and, to add a little zest to these long walks, it was not uncommon for enemy aircraft to fly low, straffing these hordes of humanity as they surged billetwards for their meals.

Of the landladies, a thousand tales could be told. One tiny old lady in Crown Street was well past the age when she should be caring for several matelots, but she felt that she had to do her bit.

Just after noon each day several hungry youths, dressed as sailors, would descend on her for their dinner; on the table they would find a large and most attractive-looking meat pie, but the snag came when she dealt out – 'Just the crust and gravy today – tomorrow the meat and veg'.

At another address, it seemed that the husband was the local coal-merchant and every morning a great shire-horse was led right through the passageway of the house from back to front, returning the reverse way in the evening. The heavy clumping of the hoofs of this great animal tended to shake the very house – but at least no one needed an alarm in that billet.

The good landladies soon became well known and were handed on from shipmate to shipmate. Upon returning to base the trick was how to get billeted into these desirable lodgings, as all the allocating was done at the base.

As can be imagined, all kinds of the most original ploys were used to get into the right billets. My favourite, after learning the ropes, was to explain to the regulating PO that I had an aunt, a Mrs Borley, living at 125 Clapham Road and she was on the Naval list of landladies and she had a vacancy. I had taken the trouble to find this out prior to arriving in the base; it usually caused raised eyebrows but it got me into a real 'home from home'.

Ma Borley, as we called her, was a quite wonderful soul. She had four children, only two of whom were living at home; the only daughter was away training to be a nurse and the eldest son was in the Army.

The house was run to her kindly but strict discipline and anyone not conforming to her standards knew that they would be reported to the base.

She had up to seven hungry sailors to feed, most of whom would be in their teens or early twenties, each with a large appetite sharpened each day by the long walks to and from the base, plus two of her own children.

Ma Borley certainly worked hard for the war effort, added to which she was at one stage bombed out of No. 125 but took up the same work in a house lower down the same road. The house, with its inmates, was always good for a laugh, and of course schoolboy Dick, the youngest of her brood, was used in the various pranks to good effect.

We ate in the kitchen, which was along the passageway and down two steps, and the front door was fitted with an old-fashioned bell-pull, which led by a wire through a series of pulleys to the kitchen. There, in an angle of the wall, it ended at a nodding bell high on the ceiling. We tied a piece of cotton to the bell and led it down the wall in the angle behind the wireless, so that a person sitting in the right position could tug at the bottom and so ring the door-bell.

Dicky would go to the door and find no one there. We did this on and off for days until in desperation Dicky took his meal into the front room to await the miscreant. Our little prank was safe until the daughter, Joan, came home on leave and, with her help, while we were all gone to the base, it was decided to spring-clean the kitchen. The tell-tale length of cotton was found. As the kitchen was in some disarray, we thought nothing of being asked to stand for a buffet-style lunch; when we were all assembled we were pelted with little paper bags filled with flour.

Flour on a sailor's navy-blue uniform is, to say the very least, a bit of a problem and we had to clean it all off before we dare appear back at the base.

The outbreak of war saw some 6,000 men passing through Lowestoft. This grew to 66,000 by the time war ended; if ever a town was bursting at the seams, it was Lowestoft.

The enduring memory of these early days was the kitting-out process. Some twenty of us were marched into the equipment store and on the other side of a long counter were twenty ratings – one for each of us.

I don't remember any questions being asked. We were eyed up and down, then from vast shelves at the rear two of each article of clothing were pushed over the counter, all to be dumped into the cylindrical sailor's kitbag. Then came two pairs of boots and all the small articles, such as hair-brush, lanyards, boot brushes, underclothes, jack-knife and, of all things, a cut-throat razor. We signed, of course, for each item. The last function was to have one's name stencilled onto the bottom of the kitbag.

Now, we were to get dressed in our newly acquired uniforms and pack our 'civvies' into the empty suitcase. To those who haven't dressed as a jolly jack, the experience is nothing short of traumatic!

Everything, it seemed, except the trousers, went on over the head and, at a later date, when this issued clothing was worn out, a new tailor-made 'tiddly' suit would be purchased from a shore tailor and made to such skin-tight proportions that it would need considerable assistance both to get into and out of. It has been known for a real 'tiddly' sailor to have to wait until a nightwatchman could spare the time to come and help him out of his well-fitting jumper.

In just a handful of days from leaving home, and without any training, I was drafted to Grimsby to join HMS *Liffy* as an ordinary seaman.

The day before I was drafted and before we had really completed our kitting-out, I was, with the rest of the class, put on a charge. It happened this way. Every Wednesday at 10 a.m. a practice mock air-raid was sounded and this was the signal for everyone to disappear below ground into the massive shelter provided. Our squad had been placed in charge of an old three-badged seaman who knew all the dodges. Having just arrived outside the padre's office for our New Testaments and balaclava helmet – our final piece of equipment – the warning went: Rather than take us all into the shelter, where no smoking was allowed, he led us round to the rear and into an old stable, where all the smokers lit up for a quiet 'burn' until the 'All Clear' went.

It seemed, however, that the authorities were well aware of this hiding-place, as suddenly the Commodore, with his entourage, appeared in the doorway. A master-at-arms took all our names and we were marched off to the ship's office. Luckily for me, before the offence could be processed I was on draft to Grimsby, so my charge sheet remained clean, a matter which at a later date proved to be of the utmost importance when I was put forward for a petty officer's course.

This was the kind of good fortune that attended me for the whole of my time in the Navy. In the days that followed I found myself drafted to good ships and from them all I made fine shipmates, which was luck in itself, for many of the men, although rough and tough from the fishing fleet, were fine seamen and they taught me a great deal which was to come in very useful in the days that followed.

My first experience of Lowestoft was a very short one; the war as far as minesweeping was concerned was urgent from the first day and I was soon to find that, being based at Grimsby, the *Liffy* would afford me plenty of seatime with very little rest in a ship working 'watch and watch'.

Dressed now as a sailor, one of the many hundreds thronging the streets, both on and off duty, one had no identity in such a place, being just one of the multitude; perhaps it was just this that made me look forward to getting off to sea.

It would be nearly twelve months before I returned to Lowestoft and in this one year I was to experience a whole array of situations that were a complete departure from my background and my upbringing.

Thereby hangs such tales as are to follow.

Chapter Three

Sea in my Seaboots

The draft said HMS *Liffy* 'to join' and the travel warrant said Grimsby – the great fishing port on the Humber.

My imagination ran away with me; what dreams there were to be dreamed of a port like Grimsby! But, sadly, in no time at all I found myself agreeing with the trawlermen themselves, who of their own river said, 'The Humber is the arse-hole of the world and Grimsby is stuffed right up it.'

Into this whole new world came Ordinary Seaman Male LT/JX 184481 and with me, as a new entry, Ordinary Seaman Harold Marriott.

When *Liffy* finally came through the dock gates and tied up alongside it was with nothing short of disgust that Marriott viewed her, for he had got it fixed in his mind that the Navy had no ships as small as this; he had hoped for something as big as the 'Mighty Hood' or the 'Nelson'.

Nevertheless, as small as she was, we were glad to see her, for we had arrived in Grimsby some ten days earlier, just in time to watch *Liffy* steam out through the dock gates for a ten-day stint at sea.

In the meantime we had been billeted in a local Salvation Army hall, where the only sleeping space available was a very dilapidated billiards table, and we had come to the conclusion that whatever *Liffy* had to offer it could hardly be worse than a billiards table with a few bugs thrown in.

Little did we know that, while it was routine for the crew of *Liffy* to sleep in warm hammocks, we were, due to the cramped conditions condemned to sleep for many weeks on locker-tops – but that was all in the future.

Despite this, and many other uncomfortable experiences yet to come, at least now we had a ship and could look forward to not having to live out of a kitbag. For the last ten days we had been wandering around Grimsby in ill-fitting, new-issue boots without a penny between us – now that would be a thing of the past.

There was no welcome on the mat for us as we dropped our kitbags aboard; this happened to be pay-day and the ship's company, having been at sea for the last ten days, were interested only in getting their pay and having a 'run ashore'. The whole of the messdeck was alive with strange men, all getting washed, shaved and into their No. 1 suits, eager for the pleasures of Grimsby.

Our hopes of getting paid vanished when we were told that, as we were not yet 'victualled' aboard, we would have to wait a further fortnight before getting our first 14s. (about 70p) less deductions and allotment. When we were finally paid we were left with £1 per fortnight, out of which we had to buy writing-paper, stamps, boot-polish and soap – the rest was spending money!'

This vast sum also included the 3d per day clothes allowance, from which we had to purchase all new clothes as required when those issued were worn out. At any kit muster you could be told to buy a new this or new that, depending on the mood of the inspecting officer. Luckily, this sort of kit inspection only occurred when we re-entered barracks.

For some years the *Liffy*, with her sister ships *Garry*, *Boyne* and *Dee*, had been based in Portland as a flotilla of fishery protection ships, but the *Liffy* was a one-off-type, having begun life as a specially built ice-breaker for the Russian navy just as the First World War broke out: she had been commandeered into our Navy and used as a dogsbody ever since.

Now here she was at war once again, sweeping the Humber and beyond, manned by Royal Navy ratings below deck and RNR (fishermen) on deck. In all but the very smallest ships in the Royal Navy, stokers and seamen lived quite apart in separate messdecks – on the basis that 'oil and water' don't mix – but on the *Liffy* we lived together.

Apart from the 'oil and water' problem, this arrangement was exacerbated by the fact that all the 'black gang' (stokers) were RN while all the seamen were RNR – and once again 'never the twain shall mix'. A further problem was evident: the *Liffy* being a coal-burner, these grimy stokers came out of the boiler-rooms still dressed in their filthy moleskin trousers, blackened singlets and sweat-stained neck-cloths, and clumped along the deck in wooden-soled Dutch-type clogs. They washed as best they could, but sitting in their stokehold gear on well-scrubbed messdeck stools did little for the understanding of the seamen, who had to scrub them.

So we had a problem without a solution! The very next day we were given further understanding of this same problem – we moved to the coaling jetty, where some 300 tons of coal were dumped on the foredeck and both stokers and seamen toiled together to get this great mass below through the bunker lids.

Depending on the amount of steaming we did, this was to become a part of our lives every three weeks or so. The first thing carried out after a stint at sea was to re-bunker ship, and this added up to being the most miserable and exhausting experience that the Navy had to offer.

After bunkering was completed the entire ship had to be hosed down from truck to keel and all scrubbed clean. When this was completed the next task was to store ship – and only when that was finished, if there was time, would any leave be granted.

Quite naturally, all new entries were given a rough time of it by the fishermen, who seemed to take great exception to we 'Hostilities Only' ratings being in what they thought to be their minesweeping navy. Our friend, however, and at the time our only friend, was Joe Sharpe the signalman; signal ratings are known throughout the Navy as 'bunting tossers', or 'Bunts' for short.

'Bunts' was RNVR and a 'Geordie' to boot. We now had this strange mixture, in a very confined space: the 'black gang' were all RN and thought themselves quite superior; the main body of seamen were RNR and didn't think much of the RN types; 'Bunts' was RNVR; and we two new entries were classed as 'Hostilities Only'.

Add to this odd mixture the dissension that goes on quite normally between the Scots and the English, throw in a Geordie or two, the North against the South and just a bit of county against county, and you have some idea of the continual strife which in fact kept us sane in these cramped, unhealthy, condensating messdecks. Yet, divided as every messdeck might seem to be, as soon as an outsider was at all critical of the ship they closed ranks to defend theirs as the best ship in the Navy.

Each day we two new entries were dealt out the most onerous of the many tedious duties. In bitter weather we stood lookout on the fo'c'sle, getting the sweep in or out; we were stationed on that part of the deck to keep us 'up to our arse in salt water'. At cleaning stations, it was always the 'heads' (lavatories), which needed a strong stomach even in calm weather.

We newcomers would have to serve a full apprenticeship, which was to last until another ordinary seaman arrived 'to join', when, with great glee, we moved up the social ladder, leaving the new boy to his fate.

The first winter of war was a bitter one and sweeping out to Spurn Point in easterly gales with thick snow falling which seemed to occur day after day, was a tough introduction to this new life.

The usual duties of lookout, in and out sweep, kept the crew on deck for most of the daylight hours – wet and cold, weary and salt-caked. In and out of Grimsby, coal ship, store ship, wash down: all these activities came and went, as did the new and devastating magnetic mine, yet while many other fine and more modern ships fell victim to this menace *Liffy*, a clapped-out old rustbucket, a survivor from the first war, survived again.

As a wartime publication at the time said:

These ships are the ones that do a great deal of hard and dangerous work and get less than their share of credit. Minesweeping may not be as spectacular as sailing into action in a battle cruiser, but it can be just as dangerous. Hundreds of these small ships are now at sea, helping to keep the trade routes open. Fishermen and members of the RNVR do splendid work in helping to man them. Some of the stories you may have heard – most of them you have not, but they are achieved every day.

And what of these fishermen? Living with them in this cheek-by-jowl situation I found, in a short space of time, that they were a very special class of men, quite apart from any other breed, fiercely proud of their calling, yet always aware that they were being exploited. When 'on', as they called them, the 'distant' fishing-grounds they worked long hours gutting fish in appalling conditions, in bitter weather, on heaving decks constantly awash with Arctic seas.

The more fish they caught the longer they had to stand there gutting them, for it seemed that having steamed 1,500 miles to these Arctic fishing-grounds it was highly necessary to begin catching that weight of fish required to replace the weight of coal burnt, otherwise the ship could become unstable.

An oilskin frock, seaboots, heavy jumper with muffler, mitten gloves and, if not a so'wester, a cloth cap. Their hands were like shovels, with marlin spikes for fingers; they knew no fear of the sea.

There was very little comfort to enjoy while at sea and they were never long enough at home to enjoy whatever comforts were obtainable there. They worked hard, they played even harder, spending up to three weeks on the fishing-grounds, with, at best, only forty-eight hours at home before returning for the next trip. Respecting only the discipline of the fist and the ultimate decision of the skipper, they were hard-drinking and generous, boastful and militant, brutalised by the job and its conditions. With little or no security, their greatest dread was to be injured to the extent that they were no longer able to go to sea; they were not covered by any National Insurance scheme and were quite unable by their very nature, of saving for the future. The sea and fishing were all they knew or cared about – but they were always dreaming of a shore job, dreams they knew, in their innermost hearts, they would never fulfil, for they came of a class of men whose bounds of attainment were only those required by the fishing industry.

To become a 'second hand', as the fishing boats call their 'mates', or at most a skipper, was the ultimate; to be anything but rough, callous and insensitive was weakness.

Mostly, they had been reared as children of desperately poor parents, with little opportunity to obtain more than a minimal education, or any social polish.

Their language was brutal, their manners non-existent, and the extent of their conversation was the ship, the sea, the skipper, women, drink and, of course, their exploits when last ashore with either or both of these last two.

When a whole race of men is bred to sail to the Arctic to catch fish in the kind of weather that only this breed can, who can be surprised that they are degraded by the experience of it?

Immediately war broke out, hundreds of them brought in from the fishing-grounds and, having already served a period of training in the RNR, straight into the Navy to fill vulnerable gaps in the country's defences. The trawlers in which these men earned their livings were, overnight adapted to minesweepers.

The largest of these trawlers became patrol vessels with some of our biggest liners up in the Iceland and Greenland gaps. Trawlers that were daily involved in earning a living in these distant northern waters made excellent patrol ships in those empty waters, through which the enemy had to pass in order to destroy our Atlantic lifeline.

This onerous task they accomplished by endlessly holding the fort in the vilest of weathers, rolling their guts out and knowing full well that, should they sight an enemy, they were expendable, though hopeful they might get the necessary sighting signal away before they were sunk!

Usually, within a week of coming in from the fishing-grounds, each was converted into a ship of war, and in so doing made more unstable by the addition of a four-inch gun and its platform on the forecastle, with numerous depth-charges added on the after casing and some of the normal bunker space converted into messdecks.

So minor, in fact, were the changes required for minesweeping that, of the week needed to convert, most of the time was taken up in slapping on the necessary coat of naval grey paint – known in the Navy as 'Crab Fat'.

Then, with quite often the same crew as she fished with, but now in the 'rig of the day', off they went to war. The majority of the crews would have been RNR ratings with their uniforms all ready at home, so almost overnight a new navy was born.

The greatest difficulty was the discipline, or lack of it. Routine and good order were things that these fishermen only had a smattering of and teaching old dogs new tricks was a slow and boring detail, especially as, in many cases, the entire ship's company, including the skipper, had fished together and had slowly to be educated into the standards required by the Navy for dress and discipline. This was complicated by the fact that immediately war broke out every last one of these ships was required at sea: consequently little progress was made by the Navy in bringing them into line with naval discipline.

There were mines to be swept, the sea-lanes had to be kept open, and vast areas of the sea had to be patrolled.

As time wore on all this was to change. Slowly the renegades and pirates were brought in from sea and packed off to naval barracks, where they were worn down until full naval discipline was installed into this former 'Harry Tate's' navy. Later, much later, 'rig of the day' would be piped and adhered-to. 'Hands to stations for leaving harbour', 'Special sea-duty men close up', 'Hands to dinner', 'Pipe down' and, of course, 'Up spirits' – all became accepted as part of the day's work.

However, these necessary changes could only be accomplished as fast as the 'Hostilities Only' officers and ratings became available and could be infiltrated into the difficult ships. The diehards whose places they took found it easier, in the long run, to comply with the required naval standards than to languish in barracks. One of them was heard to say, after a sojourn of correction in barracks, 'You might think you are a bloody good horse, but where you are going they are good jockeys.'

Gradually a new spirit arose. We were no longer the labouring force of the Navy but an accredited part of it. A special silver badge was designed and worn, with great pride, on the left cuff of our Number Ones and walking ashore with a 'HM Minesweeper' cap-tally now reflected great pride in both ship and job – but this was all a long way off yet.

Our first introduction to these impending changes was the appearance of a newly commissioned lieutenant RNVR, who took over command of *Liffy*, a well-mannered, immaculately dressed ex-banker from civvy street.

His quite different approach and quietly spoken orders from the bridge contrasted sharply with the bawdy bawlings of the skipper he had just relieved. Of course he insisted that the ship be run his way, all very much to the disgust of the fishermen; much ribald comment ensued and abuses were hurled at the bridge and the figure standing there; but suddenly we were ordered north to the Firth of Forth, though not before our coxswain (Second hands' to the fishermen) had been relieved by a much younger man, a well-dressed, stockily built PO coxswain who, although a fisherman, had accepted the Navy's standards and from his very appearance we all knew would be capable of knocking this unruly ship's company into naval shape.

Now, our trawlermen began to feel a little more hemmed-in than of late. The black gang were still all RN; the newly appointed commanding officer, as he chose to be called, was RNVR and not of the 'skipper' breed; and the new coxswain had obviously been sent to do a job. Now four of the seaman branch were 'Hostilities Only' – Marriot and I had moved one rung up the social scale!

We were not sorry to be leaving Grimsby; sailors held no special place in the hearts of its townsfolk. After all, the greater part of her men earned their bread from their toil in the sea and the womenfolk had had occasion to curse the sea for generations for taking their menfolk from them.

Even the women had over the years been made uncharitable by the sea and its effects upon their lives. They had to keep homes going while their men were away at sea for up to three weeks at a time and then, upon the arrival of their husbands' ships at the fish dock, had the right to expect a little extra money to the £2.10s per week that they had subbed from the owners.

Now, with the men back, and plenty of fish to be sold, each man would be squared up – but many a wife waited at home in vain!

The husband, with his 'square up,' which could, depending on the size of the catch, be considerable, got as far as the first pub outside the dock gates and there, with his mates and many hangers on, drank himself under the table. He was then probably robbed of any money that he might have left, and the next thing he knew he was passing Spurn Point on passage back to the Arctic. This happened trip after trip.

To say our goodbyes to Grimsby, ten of our ships company made their way to the pub of their choice and a round of ten pints was ordered by McGuinness, our biggest fisherman. The pints were due served up, but when asked for the money McGuinness had to admit that he hadn't any. Mine host did not seem to be in the least upset, having it seemed met this situation many times before – so a deal was struck. Our shipmate handed his naval oilskin and his boots over the bar and both parties seemed well satisfied. He walked back to the ship minus his oilskin and boots, but that didn't seem to worry him – this was obviously not the first time that he had been involved in such a transaction, although it was winter, with snow on the ground.

It was just before our new coxswain arrived that our ageing second hand was at the wheel, coming back into dock. Being a coal-burner, it was impossible during part of the stoking operations to prevent great billows of black smoke pouring out of the funnel. On this occasion, our new RNVR commanding officer, on the open top bridge, found himself blacked out by this smoke and in rather a pleading voice he called down the voice pipe, 'Stop making this smoke – I can't see a thing.' 'Well, strike a f–king match,' the old helmsman answered – not a remark found amiss in the fishing fleet, but not acceptable in this emerging Navy.

So 'Bradford Jack,' as the old boy was known in his home town, was relieved. They did say that in his younger days he had stolen a trawler and sailed her down to Boulogne, where he sold her and then drank the entire proceeds. He spent a considerable time in gaol following this escapade, but had no regrets. They said the fishing fleet was full of such characters.

We sailed north to Port Edgar, right under the Forth Bridge, where we learned, to our great joy, that the authorities considered the *Liffy* to be too slow and so aged, with her sweep down, that she should discontinue her active life, for the time being at least, and become one of a flotilla of training ships operating from Port Edgar.

Our entire ship's company was to tranship into the much newer and more impressive HMS *Syringa*. She was one of a flotilla of four naval minesweepers; the others were HMS *Cypress* (leader), HMS *Cedar* and HMS *Holly*.

We found it hard to believe our luck, for while sweeping in the Humber, where there had been a lot of enemy air activity, we had felt vulnerable at only four knots with the sweep out.

Chapter Four

Mr Holman's Projector

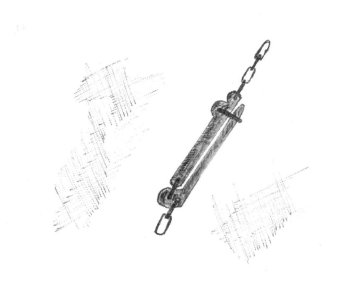

As soon as our fishermen types saw *Syringa*, they recognised her for what she was. Although far more imposing, and as smart as any naval ship could be, she had a past, and they knew it . . . It seemed that in the 1930s the fishing industry found that they were now having to sail to distant waters to find new fishing-grounds and to do this on a regular basis a newly designed trawler was needed. So this class came into being, and five of them were built.

It was found, however, that serious errors had been built into them – they 'held' too much water on the fish deck and could not free themselves of it in bad weather, so to stand gutting fish in the fish pounds in Arctic conditions was impossible. They were laid up as failures.

In 1936 the Admiralty came looking for trawlers to form into a flotilla for the Middle East, and the owners were able to cut their losses by selling all five to the Navy. To prove this it was suggested that we look behind the ship's bell in *Syringa*, where they predicted we should find her original name engraved: *Cape Kanin*. They were right.

From now on the most awful stories began to circulate. She was the most unstable ship in the fishing fleet, and must be much more so now with a four inch gun and its platform added to the forecastle; some of the bunker space had been forfeited to new messdecks and several ammunition lockers spread in various places. The yarns lengthened, until we new entries began to think that if we let go of the jetty she would turn turtle.

The best story came from an old stoker, taking me under his wing (hence the term 'old man and winger'). He confided in me that if, in bad weather, I saw the stokers putting a net over the funnel, I should take great care. When asked why, he replied that she was so bad a sea-boat the net was 'to keep the bloody stokers in'.

Now, in the much cleaner waters of the Firth of Forth, we began to shake down into a new and more efficient unit. Our RNVR commanding officer had stayed on in *Liffy* and now we had a senior RNR skipper, a braw Scott from Aberdeen. He was a man with a great presence, a man who called a spade 'a bloody spade'. A man we all learnt to respect was skipper William T. Richie RNR.

Spring was coming, and the fine days that we did get were quite superb, marred only by increasing enemy activity, the first of which was to shoot down all the barrage balloons which seemed to be holding the Forth Bridge up. This was such an impressive sight, we almost had to applaud the intrepid enemy pilot, who carried out this act solo.

Edinburgh was a simply great run ashore for all sailors. We were continually fêted, meals were paid for by the generous Scots, haircuts were free to sailors, and so were bus rides – so much for the so-called 'tight Scots'!

May Island and the Bass Rock were our sea-marks; we swept and re-swept the various channels in quite lovely weather. We polished up our sweeping techniques until we were perfect to a man: each could take over the position of any other in the deck team, until we fast became the kind of team that needed no other command than 'Out Sweep'. Competition between the four ships was encouraged and every kind of shortcut was practised.

All executive orders came from the senior ship, HMS *Cypress*, by striking the flags 'RU', meaning 'Out Sweep'. We did not wait for the order from our bridge, but immediately the flags were struck knocked out the appropriate pin and away went the sweep. In reverse, the flags 'Negative RU' were flown for 'In Sweep'; as this order meant that we had finished for the day and were homeward-bound, no time was lost in this evolution.

Suddenly, the pride had arrived. 'Action Stations', real or imaginary, were effectively carried out, even in the darkest night the whole thing came together and things began to happen as they should.

All this was merely the prelude for things to come. The flotilla now consisted of four naval trawlers commanded by a very experienced naval officer. Each of the other ships was skippered by a senior officer, with crews that were now considered to be well shaken down. Soon we were to move south, where the real action was, and we found that the halcyon days were past.

We went south to Hartlepool, and from here swept south to Sprun Point and northwards to the Tyne. A lot of coal was burnt out of Hartlepool, sweeping or keeping swept the shipping channels, for this was a busy sea-lane and continual seatime confirmed the lack of the necessary ships; we swept by day and patrolled by night, each ship run on a 'watch on, watch off' basis; over many weeks, this became exhausting.

On rare occasions, as a rest period, we were allowed to anchor under Flamborough Head. I remember during one such rest period, a lovely summer's evening, when war and all its trappings seemed to be a world away, we three – Marriott, Sharpe ('Bunts') and myself, now firm shipmates – were sitting on the upper deck doing our endless 'dohbying' (washing), when emptying the suds overboard, a trail of lobster pots was observed lying on the port quarter. All was fair game to us three pirates. But what to do about it? We decided that it would be better to wait until after dark.

The ship's boat was lying quietly astern, so at midnight we hauled in a pot or two, took out a couple of lobsters, rebaited the pots and then retired to the galley to cook this great delicacy. With the rest of the crew asleep, we shut ourselves in the wireless cabin (this was 'Bunts's' private domain) and ate hot lobster, telling ourselves that these were the spoils of war.

At dawn, working watch and watch, we were back on deck again and there, almost under our counter, was an oldish fisherman, single-handedly hauling in his pots. In a fit of conscience we invited him aboard for a cup of tea. He accepted and sprang nimbly aboard. To add to our already smarting consciences he told us that both his sons, who normally fished with him, were now in minesweepers and, as he assumed that our diet could do with a bit of a change, would we accept a couple of lobsters? With coals of fire already burning deeply into our consciences, we accepted, knowing full well that right now more lobster was more than our stomachs could carry. However, we loaded him up with duty-free cigarettes and a tot of rum for good measure. The old boy left rather confused with our generosity and the shame of this exploit still keeps its memory clear and bright to this day.

The great thing about Hartlepool was its bunkering facilities. We thought them quite unique as, instead of dumping 100 tons of coal on the upper deck to be manhandled below, an enormous elephant's trunk was placed right into the bunker lids and the whole of the tonnage required was shot into the bunker. After the backbreaking toil in the various other ports we found it hard to believe that such a simple contrivance could take so much aggravation out of a sailor's life. If only for this reason, we hoped we might spend the rest of the war working out of Hartlepool! We actually began to enjoy going to bunker, and it was not until later I joined a converted whale chaser in the Mediterranean, that I experienced the even greater advantage of bunkering with oil fuel.

The war began to change that summer. Quite often now we were being attacked by enemy aircraft in daylight and after dark the heavily armed E-boats would come out of the haze at forty knots, firing their multiple guns.

Ships in convoy were being torpedoed in daylight and, able to do at best six knots with our sweep down, we began to feel vulnerable and were aware that more, far more, small-arms were needed to fight off these sudden attacks. One four-inch gun blasting away at only one shell per thirty seconds was of little use, except as a morale-booster; we needed to be able to pour out vast quantities of small-bore ammunition, almost like a hose-pipe – but we had to wait many months before this kind of protection was made available to small ships.

All we could do was pray that the searching E-boats would choose the 'other ship' for its target, for we knew that there would be little chance for us in a direct attack.

As a stopgap, the most Heath Robinsonish contraption was fitted, a piece of what appeared to be drainpipe, about six feet long, into which pressurised steam was fed from the engine-room. This force ejected a Mills bomb which had been dropped in at the muzzle end. It was called a 'Holman Projector' – we had no idea who the inventor was, but as far as we were concerned, he should never have been let loose. The aim-off technique required to shoot down an enemy plane is difficult enough to master with a fully mobile gun able to elevate and depress – imagine now the problem, with a piece of drainpipe which had no sighting arrangements, was fitted to a heaving deck and could therefore only be pointed in the general direction of the attacking plane – which by the way, would be travelling at around 230 knots. The operator, taking all the variants into consideration, now pulled the lever and, depending on the head of steam carried at the time in the engine-room, the bomb was lobbed into the air – hopefully!

Mr Holman's 'Projector' soon became the laughing-stock of our flotilla and who better than the trawlermen, with their boisterous sense of humour, to have thought up a better way of getting practice than to hurl potatoes from this abortion at any passing ship. This piece of fun was in time to prove to be a most expensive piece of armament, for we had to pay for these potatoes from our victualling allowance.

I had by now reached the stage when, for some little time, I had quite unofficially been allowed to 'take the wheel' during watches. Finally, the leading seaman of the watch thought the time had come for me to do so officially. Addressing the top bridge via the voice-pipe, he asked the CO for 'permission for Ordinary Seaman Male to take the wheel, sir?' 'Permission granted' came back down the voice-pipe.

For the next twenty minutes I concentrated hard and thought that I was doing a fair job of the course-keeping when down the voice-pipe came the enquiry, 'Is Male still on the wheel?' 'Yes, sir,' replied the leading seaman. 'Well, tell him that I don't mind him writing his name with the ship, but don't let's go back and dot the bloody I's!'

This, I learnt later, was the standard little joke which COs played on all 'makee learners' when first they took the wheel.

About this time, Marriott and I were given an oral exam by the CO and were later informed that we were now Able Seamen. To celebrate this we went ashore together in Hartlepool – but all we could find to do with the money in our pockets was to have a haircut.

Back aboard, being still among the junior ratings, we shared all the onerous duties. Not for us the warm top bridge to clean the brasswork, or the lower bridge where the brass kept reasonable clean anyway; just the heads and helping the stoker of the watch haul up the spent ashes from the stokehold and dump them overboard.

By now the full effect of the character of the new coxswain was being felt by each and every member of the crew. He was short of stature but stockily built, observant of every detail, fair but tough, keeping us all at arms' length and coming down hard on any skiver or malingerer. If there was any part of our jobs we did not understand, then he would teach us – from then on there was no excuse for not knowing. He knew every trick in the book and every place in the ship where a man might hide – we soon learnt not to 'try it on' with Watson.

It was said of him that, just prior to the outbreak of war, while trawling in heavy weather, he had dived overboard fully clothed and saved a shipmate's life, for which he was awarded a Lloyds Medal and also received from the Prince of Wales, an inscribed gold watch. Many years later a full account of this event came into my hands; I still have it.

Summer was now with us and the lengthening days gave us no protection from the air. Day after day, either sweeping or patrolling, with even larger convoys trudging northwards, or after dark without lights, the watches were long and weary and full of anxiety lest we be hit by the lurking E-boats. So day in day out we kept up this routine and only when our bunkers were getting low were we allowed to steam for Hartlepool.

Bunkering ship was the first requirement on reaching port, followed by the drudgery of storing ship, usually from some far-off store shed. If there was time, shore leave would be granted, but usually for only one watch. This meant that six weeks could elapse before getting a run ashore. So short of ships were we in the early days – and this was only the 'phoney war'!

Daily we carried out gun drill, air-attack drill and 'abandon ship' drill. It was at such a gun drill, where we were to fire a practice round, that the gun's crew closed up rather smartly and trained the gun to a 'green' bearing, which brought the breach of the gun in line with the vertical ladder by which everyone ascended to the gun deck.

At the instant the gun fired and a large brass cartridge-case was ejected, the 'Jimmy' (First Lieutenant), who was somewhat late getting to his station, presented himself just above the platform, to be hit full in the face by the cartridge-case that has been propelled out of the breach with some force. It was not a pretty sight and we steamed smartly back to base with a very battered Number One. Our trawlermen thought this affair most amusing at the time and, as they were naturally rebellious against any sort of authority, they were of the opinion that 'If he couldn't take a joke, he ought not to have joined.'

Chapter Five

What Cold War?

Then came a whisper (these usually originated in the galley). It was a strange sort of foreign name: French, perhaps – Dunkerque.

Hurriedly we steamed south, through Dover and on to Portsmouth, which was to be our base throughout the worst of the Battle of Britain. It was here that the war proper began for us.

'Pompey' was one of the Navy's biggest bases, and we were warned by our RN personnel of what to expect – 'rig of the day', pipe ship, quartermasters at the brow at all times, saluting fifty times a day, especially when on shore leave. But there were also privileges to be enjoyed, such as having a trawler base ship, where the real comfort of a bath could be enjoyed – this, after a bucket under the fo'c'sle head, was a luxury; and Pussers stores – here we could purchase the much-prized clothes and all sorts of other gear – a large NAAFI and the city of Portsmouth, with all its delights.

Little did we know, at this stage, of the days that were to follow, and of how we were to be used over the many months for the expected invasion.

We swept through to Dover by day, then by night patrolled much nearer to the French coast than we thought prudent. Sometimes we were well inside the bombarding British destroyers, acting as some sort of a decoy and then slogging it back to 'our side' before dawn to take up sweeping stations at daylight.

There was, of course, the never-ending bunkering every time we entered port; hit-and-run enemy aircraft by day, the odd E-boat at night; and sometimes, as we neared Dover, shelling from the other side.

The memory that will never fade is of having to pick up at sea the bodies of both friends and enemy alike, and give each a Christian burial. During the Battle of Britain there were many of each to be found, so many, in fact, that we took extra firebars to sea with us to use as sinkers.

One instance stands out. The body of one of our airmen was given our rough-and-ready treatment and the name-tags recovered and passed into the base upon our return to port. Many months later we received from the grateful parents a cheque, which we paid into our mess account and out of which we bought a set of new football shirts; we were the best turned-out team in the flotilla. Such are the spoils of war.

All this time we were living in such cramped conditions that it now seems impossible that some twenty of us lived, ate, slept and shared all our recreation time in a space no larger than a normal lounge. In winter a fug built up by a small internal-combustion stove, plus the body-heat of a score of men, was indescribable. To have to get dressed, leave these conditions and go on watch in bitter winter weather was nothing less than shocking.

During the four-hour watches, each member of the watch spent an hour on the fo'c'sle as lookout and in very bad weather this could mean being 'up to your arse in cold salt water' for the whole hour. This was followed by an hour as quartermaster, at the wheel – nice and warm, comparatively speaking – then an hour as lookout aft; this was not so wet and was near enough to the galley to be able to pop in for a warm-up. The final hour was as bridge messenger. This was the best hour of all, for it meant standing quietly by and being ready to carry any messages from the CO as required and finally to call the next watch, which was done with nothing short of sadistic glee, as, providing no emergency arose, a warm and very comfortable hammock was beckoning.

Usually, about halfway through the night watches, jacket potatoes were brought round, accompanied by large mugs of ship's cocoa. These were consumed with great relish, then a further supply for the next watch was placed in the oven.

Occasionally, a particular malevolent watchkeeper would begin what at the time was intended as a joke, but as others followed a truce had eventually to be called. This not so funny joke began with the joker going into the messdeck where all off watch were fast asleep, having completed their stint as watchkeepers. Selecting a person known for having a 'short-fuse temper' he quietly shook him awake and enquired 'Do you want a piss?' then vanished back on deck and into the night.

The short-tempered victim would, at the first opportunity, reciprocate during the following night watch and so it went on. Sometimes the equally stupid question would be asked, 'Do you want to buy a battleship?' to which a better-tempered person might answer, 'Perhaps, how many funnels?' This kind of skylarking, while it may seem to be quite absurd, was in fact a safety-valve and probably kept us from going insane in these cramped, confined conditions.

One of our quite mad tricks, in order to get our own back on the leading seaman, (known as a 'killick' in the Navy, from the small anchor on his left arm which denoted his rank) who was not usually the most popular member of the messdeck, because of the job he had to do. Being also the mess caterer, at some convenient time in the evening would retire to the food store and there lay out the required number of eggs and rashers of bacon, etc. for the next morning's breakfast. This was done in order that the cook should not wake him early next morning. The cook would remove the key, open the store without waking the caterer, take out the food and cook it.

We found that the killick was a heavy sleeper, so in the middle watch the key could be inched out of its hiding-place and eggs and bacon for three cooked up in the galley. In the morning, things were found to be not quite right, with the killick swearing he had counted out correctly.

On another occasion, we found his illicit rum bottle and promptly laced it with cayenne pepper. A few days later, while convoying through Dover, we were shelled from the other side.

He went beserk and we put him ashore in a straightjacket. We never knew if it was the enemy or the laced rum that did it.

Quite suddenly, a twenty-four-hour leave was piped for all who could get home and back in the time; as all the crew except two lived in the north, this left only Ginger and me able to take advantage of this windfall.

Ginger Henderson was a three-badged AB, one of the old brigade; having done his twelve years in the Fleet, he had been called back during his seven on reserve. He had in the past been rated Leading Seaman but somewhere along the line he had 'lost his hook' for some offence. He was a messdeck lawyer and proficient in every branch of seamanship; he knew King's Regulations and Admiralty Instructions from back to front.

Very fond of his tot and of any others that might be going spare, he lived in Weymouth, so 'old man and winger' got hurriedly dressed and were able to catch the 1900 train out of Portsmouth for Weymouth.

Heavy bombing of the area had caused hours of delay and at 0600 next morning we had only reached Dorchester – and the end of the line. The kindly ticket collector informed us that a Bladen Dairies milk lorry would take us to Weymouth and half an hour later we were dropped off at the top of the esplanade, where the bandstand used to be. Two jolly jacks in greatcoats, gas-masks slung, each with a small 'diddy' case swung down the front, strode along St Thomas Street and over the town bridge. While Ginger had been on reserve, he had worked in Hope Square Brewery and as we arrived at the foot of Chapelay Steps several of Ginger's old workmates were going in to work, so, despite the fact that he had not been home on leave for ten months, he waved me a cheery goodbye with a 'See you on the 6.30 tonight' and walked with his old mates into the brewery.

As this was my first home leave since joining up, I had felt it necessary to impress my mother and sister with my ability to look after myself, and had packed my 'diddy' case with great deliberation, being careful to smooth down on the top, for all to see, a 'clean' shift of underclothes. I expected many compliments when I opened my case, which I did with a great flourish in the kitchen. My mother's first remark on seeing my work of art was, 'Oh, I'm glad you have brought your dirty washing home.'

My first day at home just flew by – I had walked to the top of Church Ope and there I found the old seafarer 'Bobby Tripe,' who regaled me with many of his seagoing tales and exploits while in the merchant navy. His final one, just to hammer home the point that, while I was dressed like a seaman, 'I had seen nothing yet', was: 'The seas aren't as big as they used to be, and the wind don't blow half as hard as it used to.'

I had the greatest difficulty in persuading my mother not to come to Weymouth to see me off and, as things worked out, what a good thing I succeeded. On entering Weymouth station, there on his hands and knees was Ginger – quite legless. It seemed that he had stayed at the brewery all day, drinking solidly, and had not even been home. His old workmates, finding from his leave ticket that he was due back on board at midnight, had taken him to the station and there I found him.

Finding an empty carriage, I was straddled across him trying to lift him in, when I was attacked from behind by a female wielding a heavy umbrella.

This turned out to be Ginger's wife and I was being blamed for getting him into this condition. All Ginger could do was dribble and laugh.

My mother would have died of shame had she witnessed this drunken scene. The journey back was as tedious as the earlier one and, upon arriving at Eastleigh, where we had been re-routed due to further bombing of the line, we had to wait an hour. Ginger had sobered up somewhat by now, but a further couple of pints – the hair of the dog – and he was legless again.

I knew that Pompey station would be crawling with RN patrols and that it was going to be a big worry getting him past their inspection. I made it past only because he was making no fuss; in fact, he was quite a happy drunk.

On now to Edinburgh Gate, only to find it shut, which meant that I had to carry him right around the perimeter of the dockyard wall – which is extensive – to Anchor Gate.

We made it back aboard just before midnight. A day or so later Ginger conceded that he had had what a matelot calls 'a good run ashore'.

For some time now, with the encouragement of the coxswain, I had been swatting to sit for Leading Seaman, spending long hours with the seaman's manual; accompanied by much ribald comment from the rest of the messdeck, I flogged away. The seamanship came almost as second nature, boats and splicing were right down my street, knotting was easy. Only Morse was a bit of a trial.

I had been at sea now for some eight months, living and working with these tough but professional RNR seamen, many of whom had been to sea all their lives and knew nothing else and yet, despite the fact that I had only a few months, the coxswain was putting me through to sit for my 'killick's' hook. I took a lot of stick from my messmates over this, for a killick, if he is to be efficient at his job, can never be popular and cannot be 'one of the boys'.

I was made to feel that I had deserted my class, but, such is the wisdom of the Navy, upon being rated the killick is drafted to another ship, where he can take a stand, having no 'old buddies' to constrain his judgements.

One fine morning we left Portsmouth early to sweep a minefield off St Catherine's Point and took the shortcut through the Solent to get there. But a summer fog caught us off Yarmouth and we anchored. A signal from the flotilla commander in *Cypress* informed me that as part of my leading seaman's exam I was to take the ship's boat away, under oars, and pull down to his ship, where I was to be deposited for what turned out to be the rest of the day.

Now, this part of our coast has an exceptional tidal system. Normally a ship is either wind-rode or tide-rode, whichever is the greater force; here, however, off Yarmouth, with a double tidal system, ships are inclined to yaw from one to the other, making it difficult to make a good 'alongside'.

Our coxswain, PO Watson, knowing this, and being intent, after all his tuition, to get his protégé off to a good start, changed out of his petty officer's uniform into that of a seaman and, taking stroke oar, sat facing me. I was now at the tiller and he gave me much-appreciated advice all the way down to the exam ship, where our every move was being observed.

We made a first-class 'alongside', considering that the job in hand was not straightforward.

Left on board for the rest of the day, I was subjected to all the various problems that the commander could find for me. I laid out, and shackled up, the entire 'Oropesa' sweep, so named after the ship on which this method of minesweeping was perfected. I spliced an eye into a wire rope, went through the procedures of bringing a ship to anchor – wheel and telegraph orders – piped a boat's crew away, and lowered the boat to sea-level. And so it went on until 'Hands to dinner' was piped. I was very glad to hear it.

After dinner, Morse and semaphore came up and finally I was

given a set of mess accounts to prove. I was glad to be told that *Syringa*'s boat had been signalled for and so at 1600 I had completed my exam.

In due course our boat arrived and I dropped gratefully aboard, feeling just a little battered by this experience, but my shipmates were better informed than I was, for the examining commander had sent in his signal 'Send boat for Leading Seaman Male'.

Now began a new set of experiences, for I knew that, having passed, I would, as soon as I was rated, have to leave all my old shipmates. In the meantime, I shared the duties of a killick with *Syringa*'s own leading seaman.

It took a short time only to be rated; in the meantime there was the same old routine: sweeping, patrolling and, of course, coaling ship.

We were under orders to sail at 1400, so, 'Hands to dinner' had been piped early, in order that we should be all squared away before we sailed. We were all sat around the messdeck, drinking the interminable tea, when our leading seaman of the mess shouted, 'No one has yet been for the fresh stores at the NAAFI!'

We were going away for possibly three weeks and to do so without any fresh goods was a serious matter. He ordered, 'Duty watch, get your skates on and get over there – here's the list.'

Marriott, Sharpe and Male were the duty watch, so off we went, fully aware that it was now 1245 and we sailed at 1400. The NAAFI was a fair way off and we cursed our rotten luck all the way there. It was hot and from the list, the amount of stuff that we had to bring back was sizeable. Fresh vegetables, bacon, eggs, sausages, liver, cheese and so on, enough for thirty men for three weeks. We arrived to find the door closed and the staff gone to dinner. It was now 1300. In utter dejection, we sat on the doorstep to contemplate the alternatives – wait until the shop opened up again, in which case we would miss the ship, or go back empty-handed.

The prospect of being at sea for three weeks with no fresh food was daunting and would not make us very popular, so in desperation we leaned back – and the door flew open!

There, neatly stacked against the wall, were the wardroom stores for the cruiser HMS *Dunedin*, all awaiting collection. In her wardroom she possibly carried more personnel than our entire ship's company, or so it appeared from the size of the pile. There were so many things that we had not seen for ages – tins of salmon and pineapple, biscuits, bars of chocolate, sardines – besides all the usual fresh goods on our order list.

We agreed that it had to be all or nothing and the prospect of being at sea with nothing closed the deal. We took the lot, loaded it onto the cart we had brought with us and hurried back aboard. We arrived when the state of tide had brought the tiny wireless cabin, which was the private domain of 'Bunts', just level with the jetty; hurriedly we stowed all the 'goodies' into this cabin, taking the remainder below.

We sailed on time and, during the following days, the three of us took turns to go along to the wireless cabin and have an unofficial tuck-in. We half-expected the RN police to be waiting on our return, but all was quiet and we never heard another word from anybody.

Air-raids, by both day and night, were becoming regular and being under orders not to man the guns while in harbour made life more terrifying than being at sea. Out there, at least, we could hit back.

After a particularly arduous patrol we returned to harbour, re-bunkered and re-stored the ship and, as some small reward for our work, our CO, off his own bat and totally contravening port orders, piped, 'Leave to watch and part' until 2200. This meant that only a token number of the crew were left aboard – the rest went ashore.

This skeleton crew consisted of the coxswain, two seamen, two stokers and a chief stoker. It so happened that at the height of a very fierce raid, around 2000 hours, instructions came from the base to clear the harbour. All ships were to proceed to sea and anchor until daylight. Our coxswain found himself in no small quandary, as he was the senior seaman rank aboard. If he obeyed this order he would be taking the ship to sea with many fewer men than were necessary for her safety. Not to obey meant reporting to the base the true state of affairs, and that would drop the 'Old Man' right in it, as he, too, had gone ashore.

We took her to sea despite the fact that at 2200 hours the leave-takers would return to find the ship missing and with no place to sleep.

With just one seaman on the forecastle and one aft, we let go, hauled off into the main stream and crawled out of the harbour with our guilty secret.

With the coxswain at the wheel, pitch black and with shrapnel from the raid hissing into the sea around us, we jockeyed, with an armada of other ships, out into Spithead. Finally we brought her to anchor and for the remainder of the night took deck watches. Only when it got too hot on deck did we retire to the galley and pots of cocoa. As dawn came up, we hauled up the anchor and, without any instructions, crept back alongside the jetty to find a much relieved CO and the rest of the crew, who had spent a most uncomfortable night in an air-raid shelter. Within minutes, it seemed, we were proceeding back down the harbour to get to sea before any awkward questions were asked.

A very valued member of our crew was Roderick Montgomery, a gentle gorilla of a man from the outer Hebrides, a quiet Christian who suffered the 'slings and arrows' meted out by his fellow messmates from the fishing ports. He took not the slightest notice of the callous taunts, or of the wet seaboots flung at him as he knelt to his nightly prayers, and eventually wore them down until in the end they all respected him for his integrity.

He had no need for the material things of this life, having been brought up in the fierce poverty of the outer islands. To exist there, one had to fish in an open boat in the Atlantic as well as farm a smallholding in the bleakest of weather. As a seaman he was superb, full of weather lore. 'Thick o' fog, flat o' calm,' he used to say. Unbelievably open-eyed at the wonder of things that we took for granted, he would gladly stay aboard and do anybody's watch rather than risk the hazards of Portsmouth.

Sometimes, however, it came to the notice of the CO that 'Monty' had not been ashore for many weeks and he would be ordered to get himself dressed and go ashore, simply to break the monotony of his existence. On these occasions he would ask if he could come ashore with us three, and together the four of us would make a beeline for the well known and much-respected 'Aggie Weston's' just outside the dockyard gates.

There he would insist on paying for the 'big eats' that every sailor makes for as soon as he gets ashore, after which he would find the largest settee in the reading-room, stretch out full length and, as he would say, 'have a nice zizz'. The three of us would then go off to the cinema and three hours later return to 'Aggies', give Monty a shake, find a fish-and-chip shop and eat our way back aboard. This to Monty was a quite memorable 'run ashore' and would suffice him for a further handful of weeks.

He had been brought up with an eye-for-an-eye sense of justice.

On one occasion, when a standin member of the crew was known to have stolen a one-pound note from a regular member of the crew, without a trace of conscience he removed the blankets from the thief's hammock, smuggled them ashore and posted them off to the home of the aggrieved sailor. He did not tell anyone what he had done until some weeks later. This was his idea of justice; coming as he did from a small community, it was easy to understand that this was the form of justice that ruled their lives.

One night, around midnight, and well to seaward of the *Royal Sovereign* lightship, flares were reported by our lookout and as, in the last few weeks, many fleeing refugees from France had been sighted, and some rescued, it was assumed that this was another such pick-up.

Closing on these red flares, we were surprised to find four enemy airmen in a rubber dinghy. Quite a swell was running at the time and we had a hard job getting them aboard; the first to try to jump and grab our gunnel missed and plunged, in all his sodden airman's clothes, right under our keel: we picked him up on the other side of the ship.

All four were exhausted, having been in the water since the previous midday, when they had been shot down by a Spitfire. The pilot was a young and arrogant German and, as he was the most severely injured, he was taken to the CO's day cabin. The other three were taken aft to the wardroom and placed under an armed guard.

Being the only member of the crew with any first aid knowledge, I was sent to the day cabin with the first-aid box. The pilot's injury seemed to be confined to his foot, but upon further inspection it was a serious one: the foot was almost completely shot away inside the flying boot. I was told to do what I could until further instructions arrived from ashore.

The first thing to do was to strip him of his wet clothes, in the process of which a high-quality flick-knife was discovered, then a Luger pistol, both of which were confiscated. In fact, although they all were brought aboard fully dressed as aircrew, by the time we put them ashore in Newhaven next morning, we had to wrap them in blankets, as all their belongings had been snatched for souvenirs.

Our arrogant enemy, after some first aid and wrapped in warm blankets, became quite boastful. It seemed he was claiming to have made an attack on and sunk a 'battleship' in Portland harbour, which, on my next leave, I learnt was the 'ack ack' port guardship, *Foylebank*. As I lived on the Island, this statement was of great interest to me, for I knew that she was a converted merchant and no battleship.

I remember, at the time I was attending to his injuries, thinking what a shame it was that one of his lovely fur-lined flying boots was damaged beyond repair, while the other one was perfect – one flying boot was no good to anyone! Meanwhile, aft in the wardroom, one of the prisoners, a truly enormous person, had begun to bleed from a wound above the hairline. It seemed that while he had been in the water the blood had coagulated, but as soon as he became warm and dry again it began to bleed. Apparently, he had thought himself to have been blinded but careful sponging-away of the encrusted blood soon exposed the fact that the wound was only superficial. He spoke perfect English, and no wonder, for he had spent some years in England and had recently taught English in a German university. We put all four ashore in Newhaven and then returned to our duties.

This was to become a night that we all talked about and argued over for many weeks. Many of us said we felt little other than a deep sense of curiosity at being so close to the enemy, others said quite openly that we 'should have let the bastards drown' – at least we had seen the enemy close up and felt a kind of pity as they were carted off to a prisoner-of-war camp for the duration.

The next time long leave (seven days) came around we were able to take with us a variety of German souvenirs. I got the Luger pistol, but at the end of the war I handed it in to the authorities – I had had enough of guns to last me a lifetime.

Many years later – in 1985, to be precise – a small notice appeared in our local free *Portland News*, asking for the company of any Portlander who had any involvement with the *Foylebank* disaster at a proposed get-together to be held at The Little Ship in Portland. I wrote the following letter:

To Mr Davies, Secretary of the *Foylebank* Survivors Society
  Dear Mr Davies
With reference to your proposed 'get together' at the Little Ship, Portland, on May 2nd, 1985.
  I am a Portlander and, at the time the *Foylebank* was sunk was serving as a Leading Seaman in HMS *Syringa*, a minesweeper based at Portsmouth.
  This of itself may not seem to have any connection with the matter in hand, but sometime in the middle watch on a not-

too-friendly night in September, following the sinking of the *Foylebank*, flares were reported in mid-channel well to seaward of the *Royal Sovereign* Lightship.

We closed and found four German airmen in an inflatable raft and rescued them.

The crew of this ditched bomber had only minor injuries, but the pilot, an arrogant German, had his foot shot away and, being the only member of the crew with any first-aid knowledge, I was sent to the CO's cabin to attend to his injuries.

It transpired, among his many boastings, that he claimed to have sunk a battleship in Portland Harbour earlier in the summer and from my enquiries made when next on leave, his claim would seem to be substantiated, as he described in detail the attack exactly as it happened.

This personal experience came vividly back to me when reading of your intended reunion and as we put our captives ashore next morning in Newhaven, to spend the rest of the war as prisoners, I sometimes wonder if this pilot could still be alive and, if he could be traced, what an interesting guest he would make at some future reunion – if only 'To honour when we strike him down the foe that comes with fearless eyes'.

Yours faithfully

I received the following letter from Mr Davies.

Dear Mr Male,

I was very pleased to receive your letter and your experience in rescuing the four Germans who had been shot down in the Channel, also of your suggestion of inviting the German pilot who attacked us.

About four years ago I was offered the names and present addresses of the Germans and put the idea of inviting them to our reunion to our committee, but I'm afraid I was shot down and in no way would the members agree to the idea.

However, I still receive news of them and was recently told that one of them had died about six weeks ago.

Yours sincerely

Peter Davies

I attended this meeting, along with about forty of the *Foylebank's* survivors, and took along with me Mr George Bollen, who at the time of the sinking was chief engineer in the dockyard tug *Pilot* and did valiant work in getting alongside and taking off many survivors.

Activity over the Channel was now endless both by day and by night and although we saw many more ditched airmen, these were the last we picked up alive.

In this same September of 1940, when the invasion of England seemed imminent, we left Portsmouth on one of our regular sweep-by-day, patrol-by-night beats. By day we swept from the *Royal Sovereign* lightship eastwards to within spitting distance of Dover; at night we found ourselves patrolling westwards along the French coast.

The purpose of trailing our coat close to the French coast was so that advanced warning could be flashed to our base should we find that the long-expected invasion had begun. The codeword to be used was 'Blackbird' should we find the invasion 'on its way.'

The only member of the crew outside the CO who was aware of the importance of the use of 'Blackbird' was 'Bunts,' our signalman.

On all these occasions we were briefed to keep a sharp lookout at all times; being near to the enemy coast only served to add to the tension. On this particular night, in the middle watch – pitch black, as I remember – our lookout reported a strong smell of what seemed to be paraffin.

'Action stations' were sounded and certainly the smell of paraffin seemed to pervade the whole ship. 'Silence on deck' was ordered and in the blackness of the night our imaginations took over.

The order to transmit 'Blackbird' was given and, having carried out our duty, we retired to our dawn sweeping stations, expecting all the time to see the German invasion fleet come over the horizon.

Later in the day we were recalled to base, to find that the whole affair was an exercise or 'dummy run'. Our CO had in fact been instructed to send the codeword, as it was thought by the authorities ashore that our troops standing by to repel the invasion had been 'stood to' for so long that they had become a little rusty and needed to be sharpened up.

The paraffin we thought we had smelled must have been a suggestion triggered off by the tenseness of the situation.

More men were now becoming available and soon, additional seamen arriving aboard, we were able to work the ship in three watches, not the wearisome two that had to date governed our lives.

More armaments, too, became available. We now had a pair of Lewis guns on each wing of the bridge and word had it that shortly we were to get a set of the point five twin guns to be fitted to the top of the galley.

With the extra men came easier watches but at the same time our already overcrowded messdeck became even more congested, until it seemed that this intolerable situation could only, in the course of time, cause the ship to burst at the seams. But soon now the time would come to move on – to leave *Syringa*. I began to wonder just what the future had in store for me, for while I had cursed the ship many times in the past, now that the time had come to part company with so many of my shipmates, I knew that there would never be another ship quite like this one.

Throughout this whole period the one individual in the messdeck who had commanded my greatest respect and with whom I still keep in touch was 'Bunts' – Joe Sharpe, from the Tyne – agile of mind and quick to laugh. Due to the great shortage of his rating he carried out both the duties of signalman and wireless operator, which put him in the unique position of being the first person in the ship to receive, decode if necessary, and pass on all signal to the CO.

He was privy to all incoming and outgoing signals affecting our daily lives – he knew, for instance, how much leave was to be piped and for how long we were to take in stores, from which we could deduce how long we would be away. When we were due for a boiler clean, he knew all about everything and, being the joker that he was, he was not averse to a concoction of 'buzzes' – just for the damn of it.

I was usually brought into his pranks, as was Marriott. The result of this, apart from and being close friends aboard, was that we invariably went ashore together, always providing that 'Monty' would 'stand in' for one of us.

As the fishermen had given us a rough time in the early stages, we were now part of every plot and device to get our own back. By virtue of his superior intelligence, 'Bunts' was endlessly taking the mickey out of our fishermen shipmates. One in particular was quite illiterate and very happy with that state of affairs until he came to writing home to his equally illiterate wife. This the three of us undertook to do for him, and quite blithely copied out extracts from the amorous love letters of Anna Karenina and posted them off to his wife in Hull. It seemed to work well at that end, for the unfortunate wife had to enlist the help of one of her neighbours, who must have seen the funny side of the situation and wrote back in equally amorous terms to the husband, who had to pass letters over to us to read to him. We read to him the kind of letter that we expected he would receive from an illiterate wife, not the amorous composition.

With the distance of years, this now seems to be a very unkind sort of joke, but at the time it proved to be just the safety-valve we all needed.

With his nimble mind, 'Bunts' could, and often did, start off all kinds of arguments in the messdeck. Having given them a good push to get them started, he would vanish to hide in the wireless cabin, leaving a simmering division in the messdeck. An hour or so later he would re-appear, give the problem another stir and vanish again. These arguments could go on for days.

Never a more 'tiddly' sailor ever stepped ashore. No issue overcoat for him but a smart 'pussers' Swallow raincoat and buckle shoes, long jumper tapes and a very smart bow to his cap-tally. He had rather a good singing voice and, in a sort of harmony, we sang the much-loved sea-song, 'Larboard Watch Ahoy':

> At dreary midnights cheerless hour
> Deserted even by Cynthia's gleam
> The weary sailor tired and worn
> Clings tightly to the weather shroud
> And sings as he views the gathering clouds
> 'Larboard watch ahoy!
> 'Larboard watch ahoy!

It was he who stuck up in the wheelhouse the evocative text proclaiming: 'He who sends the storm guides the ship'.

One can easily imagine the ribald remarks that this small text was apt to draw from any hard-pressed quartermaster struggling to keep a good course in a quarterly sea. In all he was a great shipmate, not perhaps if you were on the wrong end of his pranks, but as we could not beat him we joined him. Every ship should have its 'Bunts' – he kept us alive through the drudgery that can be the seaman's life; he irritated us all at times; he made up little instruments of torture; and it was plain that one had to be on his side or suffer the consequences. He played the mouth-organ well and his cooking was much better than our official 'boy' cook.

He had the ability to have gone much further than he did, but was held back by the fact that he was in a specialised branch of the Navy, where throughout the war there would be a shortage of good operators, 'one-offs' in small ships, treated like gold-dust, and therefore often passed over when promotion came up.

His perfect foil was Marriott, intelligent and with the very best of backgrounds, highly fluent and articulate, with a great sense of humour. He seemed to be completely indifferent to the money he had been so used to. Untidy in the extreme, he was so very adaptable and loved slumming it in the lowest pubs and dives. He tried, vainly, to exist on a matelot's pay, as both 'Bunts' and I had to do, and found the living in these conditions quite foreign to his upbringing, but he decided to immerse himself in this new experience – at least until it hurt, then, unlike the rest of us, he could extract himself from being perpetually broke by having the family bale him out. The foul language that he loved to use came awkwardly from his cultured voice, for his adjustment to this quite harsh standard of living had been incomparably greater than any of the rest of us.

The first time he arrived back from leave, having been deposited at the dockyard gates by a Daimler, we saw him coming down the jetty towards the ship and we all recognised that 'something was wrong' with this oncoming sailor.

It turned out that, on arrival at his home, he had taken off his uniform and not until he was due back did he put it on again. In the meantime, the maid had picked it up from the floor where he had left it and in the only way that she knew had pressed his bell-bottoms with the usual 'civilian' crease right down the centre of each leg. Little did she know that in the Navy we had seven *horizontal* creases.

Great hampers of 'goodies' used to arrive for him, all of which he shared with the messdeck. He never got into the routine of having so much stew served up for dinner and on these occasions each member of the crew would have two dumplings placed in the stew for him, and if anyone fancied a sweet for his 'afters' then he took a dumpling out of the stew, scraped off any gravy and generously covered it with jam. It saved a lot of washing up!

On a rota basis it became the turn of every seaman to do a week as messman to the petty officers' mess. This meant that he saw to the preparation of the POs as to what they had for their meals and on one occasion it was decided that for their sweet they would have what the Navy call 'figgy duff'. Now, never in his life had Marriott even boiled an egg, so after getting up all the ingredients from the store, he mixed them all up and took the result along to the cook; all he had to do then was to fetch his concoction and serve it up. The result was inedible, in fact uncutable, and in disgust the POs covered it with boot polish and it served to keep the wheelhouse door back for many weeks.

By now the greater part of the ship's company had been together for getting on for a year and no doubt the powers-that-be thought it time to move some ratings on to specialise in other courses, now that they were experienced seamen. Marriott was recommended for a commission and left us to join a minelayer in which to do his two month's probationary period. During this short spell his ship was blown up in a minefield and he was injured and spent the rest of the war in Lowestoft doing office work. Such are the fortunes of war!

My draft arrived shortly afterwards. Little did I know that when I said goodbye to *Syringa*, I had also said goodbye to minesweeping – my future was to lie elsewhere.

The following appeared in a book called *The Silent Victory*, by Duncan Grinnel Milne.

. . . it must be remembered that there were others more obscure, who at this time were tried to the limits of endurance, those whose toil was often unceasing by day and for whom the night brought no respite – and not least those in minesweepers and small ships who at all hours and in all weathers held the seas.

Normally our officer compliment was two, the CO and the 'Jimmy' or second-in-command. For a short time, however, we were joined by a third officer 'for instruction'. Oddly enough, although coming for instruction, he was, being a two ringer (lieutenant) senior to our own CO.

He was, we soon found out, not of the fishermen breed but a deep-sea man and his background, when compared with that of our 'skipper,' allowed us to watch a very interesting experience unfold. The basic problem stemmed from the fact that deep-sea men spend probably ninety-five per cent of their seatime out of sight of land, whereas our fishermen type are at home 'smelling' their way, even in thick fog, along the heavily used shipping lanes around the coast.

Wartime, of course, compounded these normal risks, as no navigational lights were shown along our coastline and it should be remembered that we had none of the sophisticated navigational aids that are commonplace today.

So, here we had a deep-seaman trained in every branch of seamanship, but unused to constant inshore work, in a ship that was so small that it bore no relationship to the ships in which he had been trained, who found himself in charge of the ship in pitch-black conditions with no lights to help him.

It was not surprising that in the wheelhouse below the bridge we could feel the tension of the man above, who for the next four hours was in charge of our lives – more especially when we were close to the French coast.

His 'for instruction' period lasted only a short time and, as decent an officer as he was, there was a queue to help him ashore with his bags when he finally got his next appointment.

On one occasion, a fine morning, HMS *Syringa* was sweeping in the company with HMS *Reboundo*, when we sighted, coming in to attack, a Junkers 87 flying at about 300 feet. Our challenge was met with a burst of machine-gun fire, and, as the plane passed over *Reboundo*'s quarter, a salvo of bombs was dropped.

Reboundo's twelve-pounder gun went into action, and it was then our turn. Our upper decks were sprayed with machine-gun bullets and two more salvos of bombs were dropped, one to port, one to starboard. Both missed us. The plane went back to attack *Reboundo*, injuring her skipper. Again returning to *Syringa*, its rear-gunner killed seaman Collier at his Lewis gun.

As the plane passed over, a bomb pierced the engine-room casing, crashed down on the platform at the fore-end of the engine, but failed to explode.

The Junkers circled and returned for a third attack, but it seemed to be losing height and dropped down within range of our four-inch low-angle gun. Two well-placed shots sent the German into the sea a mile away. I'll always remember how naked it felt to be on the gun platform under these conditions.

Our CO, skipper W. Richie, a braw Scot, went down into the engine-room, where, despite the presence of an unexploded bomb, Chief Stoker Clinton and Petty Officer Woods had remained at their posts. With the help from the skipper, these two carried this heavy bomb up a near-vertical ladder to the deck and dropped it derisively overboard, for which the skipper was awarded the DSC and the other two DSMs.

A signal instructing us to land our dead gunner at Newhaven soon arrived and, once again, being the only 'first-aider' in the crew, I was instructed to prepare the body as best I could for the journey ashore.

We steamed into Newhaven at what must have been low-water spring tides, for I remember how diminutive it felt to be alongside so towering a jetty and how difficult it was to hoist the loaded stretcher from our deck up to the top of the jetty.

On a suitable cart, provided for us, four of us took our late shipmate through the town and said our goodbyes in the local mortuary, then, still in a state of shock, made our way back aboard. We sailed immediately.

Some days later, with depleted bunkers, we returned to our base at Portsmouth. There awaiting us was a letter from the widow of our gunner, requesting that her husband's wedding ring be returned to her, as she had been told at the mortuary that it was not on the body when we left it there.

This letter not only saddened but shocked us, for we all held our gunner in great respect and were sure that when he left the ship the ring went with him.

The hole that the unexploded bomb made in passing through the casing now needed some repairs and, much to our surprise, we were directed to a berth away from our normal 'mother' ship (HMS *Marshal Soult*) to a much more imposing one close to a 'County-class' cruiser.

At this unusual berth we learnt that, in a few days' time, by a strange coincidence, His Majesty King George VI was due to inspect units of the Fleet and that we, with our bomb hole proudly evident, had arrived in time to get ourselves scrubbed from truck to keel to become a showpiece for his inspection.

We scrubbed and polished, above and below decks, hours and hours of it – knowing full well that immediately after the visit we would move out to the coaling lighter and have tons of coal dumped in the well-deck, all to be shovelled aft under the boat into the bunker.

The King did inspect us, with a whole entourage of followers. At the time there seemed to more VIPs on the upper deck than there were ships company. Standing tall among this throng was the Admiral of the Dockyard, known to all as Admiral 'Bubbles' James.

Sir 'Bubbles', it seemed, had in early childhood 'sat' for what was to become the famous 'Pears Soap' advert, a small boy dressed in a velvet suit, with a mop of curly hair, blowing bubbles. This advert had gone around the world and the name of 'Bubbles' had stuck, as well you might imagine it would, throughout his naval career.

He still had a mop of curly but now white hair, which protruded from under his cap in a rather unruly manner, so much so that one of the more irreverent members of the messdeck said that if he as a seaman had dared to walk around needing a haircut so badly, he would have been awarded seven days' stoppage of pay and leave.

The King, in Admiral of the Fleet's uniform, inspected us as a ship's company, and had a special word for our CO and the engine-room staff who had hauled the bomb up from the depths and dropped it overboard. None of us had ever seen so much gold braid before.

An hour later, we were all in our working rig and alongside the dreaded coaling lighter – after the Lord Mayor's Show!

Our CO, as can be seen, was a man to be reckoned with. One member of our crew was a bit of a 'skate' who on every occasion would dodge work by pretending to be sick. On one particular morning he had asked to see the CO, and being at sea did so on the bridge, where, not for the first time, he put his case. I was at the wheel on the deck below and down the voice-pipe I got the following: 'Now, you go away and turn in your hammock, sonny – it takes a man just fifteen minutes to die. If you aren't dead in fifteen minutes, get back on this bloody deck!'

Chapter Six

Back to Base

My draft when it came, was back to Lowestoft, after an absence of nearly a year. What changes had been wrought: the whole place was alive and as 'pusser' as the barracks at Chatham. A commodore was in command. Small in stature was Daniel De Pass, but as a senior officer he stood tall.

Each man was still billeted in private digs, but the base had now adopted the foolproof system of colour cards and no man could now go absent with impunity. The ship's company now wore the usual webbing and gaiters, and no one wandered around aimlessly.

As a leading seaman I found that I now had a choice of joining a course in either asdics or gunnery. I chose gunnery, as I found a four-hour watch at an Asdic set highly boring. This choice took me back to Chatham, with all its early memories.

While packing my kitbag in *Syringa*, I found myself doing it with a very heavy heart. I had at times cursed the old ship, and had on many occasions prayed for a draft chit, but now that it had arrived I found that I was facing an unknown future. With the old ship, we had seen a great deal of seatime together and a fair bit of action – and this is the stuff of which shipmates are made.

For the whole of the period of the expected invasion, we had been stationed in the most vulnerable part of the Channel at a period of history when the danger of this island being invaded was at its greatest and both ships and men were run ragged. During the Battle of Britain we had carried out the onerous task of picking up, and burying at sea, both our own and the enemy's dead. We had swept and convoyed by both day and night and had patrolled the French coast at night. On return to harbour we had the accursed coal to contend with.

The Navy, as was to be expected, had taken a firm hand on things at Lowestoft and were showing that they intended to keep it that way. Immediately upon entering the gate each rating began what is known as 'joining routine.' This meant, as always, a kit muster. All naval ratings were paid a daily clothing allowance; however small this was, a rating was expected to keep his kit in good order from it. Going into barracks was as good a place as any to check up on whether he was doing so, hence the muster.

The next event was doctor's examination. Here again the usual long queues developed. The memory of a room full of naked, pallid men all waiting for the usual inspection still lingers. Then on to the dentist, and more queues – not as devastating an experience, as at least you remained fully clothed.

Next, the ship's office, where each sailor was matched against his official records, which were brought up to date. Here my documents informed the authorities that I was overdue leave, and off I went the following morning for ten days.

On my return, I was told that, until the next gunnery class was made up, I should join the ship's company and became leading seaman of the guard, a job I soon learnt to hate intensely, as I found myself completely out of my depth, having so far spent my entire time at sea, with none of this 'spit and polish'.

It was in this capacity that I found myself responsible for the prisoners in cells. Part of that duty was to look in on every occupant once every hour to see that all was well. Imagine my horror when, looking in on a 6' 7" Norwegian, I found that he was trying to hang himself with his braces; being so tall, however, he had not allowed for the stretch of the elastic and while he was rapidly going blue his heels were touching the ground.

General panic ensued and a long investigation followed; explanations and reasons were required as to why the prisoner had been allowed to retain his braces. I began to wish I had never left *Syringa*.

While here I learnt that any rating was allowed to ask to see his Certificate of Service, so at the ship's office I was somewhat taken aback to find the report of my Leading Seaman's examination by Commander Lawson RN, and the shattering comment: 'Leading Seaman Male has passed a good examination, do not recommend that he be promoted further due to impediment in his speech. (I was a stammerer.)

Just a few days later I joined the gunnery class that I had opted for and was again *en route* for Chatham.

Over many generations, since Nelson and perhaps long before that, the dangerous art of gunnery and the consequent handling of high explosives in their various forms had caused many accidents in the Navy. From each of these accidents, usually costing many lives, much experience had been gained and it was this experience that was about to be passed on to every gunnery candidate in the form of the 'gunnery drill'.

The whole essence of this drill was the Navy's own brand of discipline. In the days that followed each class would be drilled to such a degree that the principles which the course sought to impress on them would not be forgotten for the rest of their lives.

Each class had its own instructors, known as GIs (Gunnery Instructors), each of whom had been specially selected and was either a chief or a petty officer and fearsome by nature.

Every day began with a session of small-arms drill and each man was badgered, cajoled, threatened and bludgeoned in the most pugnacious way.

Up and down an enormous parade-ground we went, legs, feet, arms and backs aching until they burned; the slightest error on anyone's part and everybody was sent to double around the vast perimeter of the parade-ground, jogging away in full pack and gaiters, with rifle held at arms' length, until the GI thought we had learnt the lesson – and all this in heavy studded boots, with feet made tender by having been at sea for nearly a year, where either seaboots had been the 'rig of the day', for working on deck, or, if going ashore, we had worn light walking shoes.

Little relief came at 'stand easy' as, if a cup of tea was needed, we had to double away to the NAFFI, usually to find that the whole of the ship's company was there before us in the queue and by the time 'carry on' was sounded we were not even in sight of the serving-hatch.

This was possibly where many non-smoking candidates took up smoking, in quiet desperation, with feet painful with blisters, finding a convenient wall and squatting on their heels to ease their frustration with their first-ever 'fags'.

This temptation passed me by, as I didn't think I could have found the energy to have struck the match to light the fag!

Each day was broken up into four sessions, two before noon and two after, with each session separated by a 'stand easy'. At this point we had a change of instructor and subject. Even in class we sat at attention and all ranks below that of leading seaman had to move at the double when crossing the parade-ground. This was a reminder of the now long-gone day when, from a small knot of disgruntled sailors who had collected on the parade-ground, a full-scale mutiny had developed.

Not having to run in this situation was looked upon as a great privilege. The other was not having to take part in the washing-up in the mess; 'when you get the hook you don't take cook' was the phrase used to remind juniors of one's exhalted rank.

Never, in the waking hours, was a rating out of the watchful gaze of patrolling GIs. Correct 'rig of the day' was essential, cap on straight, jumper pulled down and boots well shone; collars were minutely inspected to see if the three white lines were spotless, and woe betide any rating who had borrowed a collar and its name did not tally with that in his paybook.

Any departure from the rules brought swift punishment: loss of pay and free time, extra work in the dog watches or stoppage of shore leave. All these were legitimate punishments but a whole variety of quite unofficial punishments were possible if any GI was crossed – running round the parade ground carrying a six-inch shell, for instance, or marching alone with a rifle held at arms' length, a physical torture enjoyed not only by the GI but usually by the rest of the class. It was all part of learning to do just what you were told when you were told to do it. It was as simple as that!

In class we were told of the various accidents that had occurred in ships at sea and always the accent was put on the fact that they had happened because someone had *not* done what he had been told, when he'd been told to do it. We heard about what could happen if the temperature in the magazine was not kept under control, and the need for regular checks, or what happened if a breech-block was not properly shut.

Thus we learnt that discipline was all-important. 'Don't criticise, just obey' was the slogan.

It was while we were in class that the quite stunning news of the loss of HMS *Hood* came to us – the 'Mighty *Hood*', as she was fondly known in the Navy. It was hard for we 'Hostilities Only' types to fully understand the enormous affection with which this particular battle cruiser was held throughout the service. We saw rum-swilling, tobacco-chewing matelots with tears in their eyes at this great loss to the Navy.

Off-duty hours were spent in study in the well-scrubbed messdecks, where at 1900 hours every night, and at a given bugle-call, 'night clothing' would be adopted. This meant that all off-duty ratings would remove their white-lined collars, leaving only those on duty watch wearing collars which, should they be required for any work, made it easy to pick them out in the messdeck.

At 2100 hours the officer of the watch, preceded by a bugler sounding 'G', would inspect the messdeck before 'pipe down' and each man seated would spring to attention and remain so until the officer had passed and the 'carry on' had sounded. Only then could we relax again.

After many days of this apparently needless and heartless discipline we began to see the light and to understand just what all this was about.

A sort of love hate relationship began to develop between the elation of being in a well-trained gun team and the sheer physical pain that it engendered. At gun drill as a consequence of continual badgering, the team began to look like a team and soon, by dint of endless repetition, each member of the gun's crew could take on the duties of any other. Blistered feet soon became hardened and the back and arms ceased to ache as in former days.

Living in barracks was an experience in itself and one never to be forgotten. At the time, there actually seemed to be ratings who liked living in these conditions and who thrived on it and were part of every fiddle. They knew the rule-book inside out and, what was more important, they knew how to get around the rules.

They knew, for a price, how to obtain free railway warrants and could sell rationed 'nutty' (chocolate). These ratings were known as 'barrack stanchions' and counted it a dire failure if their names appeared on any draft chit, whereas for most of the ratings getting back to sea was a priority.

This they could not explain or understand, for the whole of the time they were out there at sea they cursed it and wished they were back in the safety of barracks.

It seemed also that the Navy was split into two distinct groups. There were the 'big ship' men and those who preferred the 'boats' (destroyers). Each group spoke in friendly disdain of the other. 'Battle wagons', or 'slab-sided bastards' was what the destroyer men called the big ships, and with equal contempt the 'big ship' men referred to destroyers as 'boats.'

For the whole of our time at Chatham we had to scramble, every night to find a billet for our hammock in the infamous 'Tunnel' (a vast air-raid shelter), where for safety's sake every rating other than ship's company had to sleep. The form was that, as soon as class had finished, we all scrambled to our mess, where we would collect our hammock and with it make for the Tunnel. The mouth of this great cavern was not the safest place to be in an air-raid, but cheek-by-jowl inside, the air became so fetid that sleep was impossible and the 'wakey wakey' bugle was welcomed.

During the second week of the course the class was suddenly interrupted and any rating standing six feet tall in his boots, of which I was one, was told to report to the equipment store: beginning the next day, I would miss gunnery instruction. We were equipped with full parade kit, webbing, gaiters and rifle. No explanation was offered, we just had to be there in our best No. 1 suits. The air was full of conjecture as to what this was all about.

Each day we drilled and drilled and no one bothered to enlighten us. Some ratings were weeded out and returned to their classes; the remainder were subjected to more drilling and marching, rifle drill and spit-and-polish.

Anyone who has not experienced this sort of work up can have no idea of the sheer physical and mental punishment perpetrated upon each member of the squad finally selected. Soon the normal webbing was exchanged for white and each of us was supplied with a white-topped cap, which had been withdrawn for the duration of the war; and still we drilled.

It was now obvious that we were to be some sort of guard of honour, but still we were not told. We drilled and drilled and marched and marched, presented arms, ordered arms, on and on, day after day, while we were fumed and cursed at by the GIs.

When the GIs turned out in their best No. 1 suits, we decided that we must be getting near to the final stages, and now our master-at-arms carried a cutlass and the officers joined in.

We next marched with a royal Marine band and, the final touch, the hallowed Royal Naval Colours were carried at the head of the squad. We learnt at last, that were to be a guard of honour at a war weapons week in London – still some seven days away, and still we marched!

Every day now there was a full-scale mock-up of the march-past, with senior officers taking the salute on the dais. Every day now our love hate relationship grew in intensity. We cursed our rotten luck in having passed through this weeding-out process. But, oddly enough, as we cursed we also gloried, if secretly, at the back-breaking slog of being in a well-drilled squad.

Let no one underrate, as they watch such a squad on the march, the pure blood, sweat, toil and tears that have gone into its making; but the curses which lead up to the parade are long forgotten, all that remains is the pride in being able to boast that 'I was there'.

The classes now resumed, I finally passed out as a gun layer, class 2 and was sent back to Lowestoft.

Glad as I was to see the back of Chatham, in retrospect I had lived through the punishment of a gunnery course, lived with 'big ship' men and had listened to their tales, slept in the infamous tunnel and most of all had survived this famous parade-ground and all it could throw at me.

For the journey back to Lowestoft, as senior rating I was put in charge of the draft of some twenty men and made responsible for the safe keeping of all documents, rations for the journey and the delivery of twenty bodies to Lowestoft. It is amazing how many things seem to go wrong on such journeys. Men go to the lavatory and don't come back, men talk to girls and forget the time, and so it goes on – it's rather like trying to get a flock of sheep through London at rush-hour; I was glad to finally report twenty men all correct back at base.

Once again I found myself back in the guard, but not for long. My name was piped over the tannoy system and I found that I was to attend a selection board, with Commodore De Pass sitting as president, with several other senior officers. Somewhat bewildered, I lined up with a dozen other leading seamen in a dark, forbidding passageway, awaiting an audience with the great man.

This was the first time I actually talked to a man with so much gold braid on his sleeve, but I found the experience not too bruising once I had found out the reason for my being there.

It would appear that I had arrived back at base at a most propitious moment. Many of the minesweeping-type of vessels were being lost to the deadly new magnetic mine and because of this there would be a dirth of petty officers in the days ahead. All leading seamen were being interviewed, providing they had a clean record – shades of my being on a charge, but having escaped on draft before it could be processed – for potential petty-officer qualities.

The interview was thorough and full of detail, none of which seemed to have much to do with the Navy. Had I been a boy scout? 'If so, had I been a patrol leader'? 'Could I swim?' (In view of my being here because of the loss of so many petty officers, I thought that a bit rich.) 'What sports did I play?' 'Why had I joined the Navy?' and so on. I was sent out of the room while my service documents were discussed.

Later in the day I was informed that I had passed the selection board for the petty officer's course, which would be commencing within the next ten days. In the meantime, I was told to report to the navigation school.

The navigation school was held in the town, in itself great news, as it meant that the long, tedious walk to the base was no longer necessary; if only for ten days or so, this was a great boon.

I enjoyed those few days very much. The instructor was a fatherly old seadog locally known as 'Skipper Balls'. I remember very well the occasion when he was checking through a student's chart work on the Thames estuary. He suddenly ordered the pupil to 'stand to attention and take your bloody cap off – from my reckoning you are in St Paul's Cathedral!' One of his little jokes that we remembered and told over and over again.

These days at school passed all too quickly, for the next phase was concentrated on the more advanced subjects from Part Two of the manual of seamanship. We had talks on the power of command and lectures on naval history, discipline, organisation and seamanship until it ran out of our ears. Paperwork was considered to be of the utmost importance – how to keep up to date with the mass of forms. This particularly applied to the victualling side of things – the issue of rum and loaned clothing and how to exchange it. It seemed that there was a form for everything and, providing the right form was used, any problem could be overcome.

Wireless telegraphy and coding were packed in to the six weeks and of course we marched and did rifle drill; but having just completed a gunnery course at Chatham this was a doddle.

Suddenly it was all over and I has passed out and would be drafted as a petty officer coxswain and probably never use my gunnery rate again (little did I know). At this point I was granted ten days' leave and told to stitch on all my correct badges, as this was foreign-service leave.

How I would have loved now to have been able to meet Commander Lawson RN – if only to remind him of his comment on my passing out leading seaman: 'Do not recommend that he be promoted further due to impediment in speech.'

I remembered how incensed I had felt on first reading this comment and that I should be condemned because of it. Perhaps I should thank him for making me 'bloody-minded' enough to want to break the endless chain that is the lot of a stammerer. Stammering gives you an inferiority complex and you have an inferiority complex because you stammer.

Back now again in Lowestoft. The 'buzz' had it that we would be going to Iceland. This was the draft to be feared. Of all the places on this earth, Iceland had the worst reputation. Its weather was abominable – endless gales, long dark winter days and cold.

There must be some joker in the Navy who spends his time inventing these rumours, for the coming days brought inoculations and even pith helmets, with a full set of tropical kit. All this was carried out with the greatest secrecy, added to which we were kept in the base, sleeping on the floor of the large concert hall.

However, on the day of our departure, the whole draft, some 104 men, was marched to the town station, headed by a Royal Marine band.

Chapter Seven

Troopship Experiences

We joined an ancient three-funnelled troopship called the *Empress of Asia*. She must have been long overdue in the knacker's yard, and all this was not aided by the fact that we joined her on an absolutely filthy November day in Liverpool.

Here began an experience which over the years has not dimmed – by far the most deplorable episode that my wartime service had to offer.

It is quite understandable that, during wars, many sacrifices have to be made, and I suppose herding together 8,000 troops in a ship designed to carry 800 passengers is one of them. I am sure that any of the many thousands transported during the war would agree that the experience was far below that required for human dignity. It was horrific.

Almost all the naval draft had been serving in minesweepers and had become used to cramped and uncomfortable living quarters, with impossible sleeping conditions, but that was near-perfection compared with what was now on offer. Way down on 'E' deck in the North Atlantic winter, conditions were grim but were to become even more unbearable when we reached the tropics.

To the stench of closely packed human beings as they lay in their own vomit can be added the shortcomings of a sanitary system designed for 800 fare-paying passengers, but now being used by 8,000 troops; and the whole of this while tumbling around in a rustbucket of a ship; rolling her way through a North Atlantic winter, with every rivet groaning and all her plates creaking.

Mealtimes, as we swung north towards Iceland, were in themselves an experience; long queues, insufficient cutlery and china, a hopelessly over-burdened catering staff and the kind of food that you ate because you were hungry, not because it was attractive or well presented.

Oh, to be back in *Syringa*! But there was, as there always is, a lighter side. We matelots had great fun and games showing the mass of soldiers first how to sling a hammock, then how to get into it and finally how to sleep in it – the whole thing was hilarious, and never seemed to end.

The art of the successful use of a hammock seems to be known only to a sailor; a soldier in a hammock is about as ridiculous as a sailor on horseback. At or about 'lights out' we toured the vast messdecks and helped hundreds of soldiers into what for them was a most awful death-trap.

All troopships during the war were run by the Army and in this instance the presence of the Navy was just about tolerated, but inherently the Navy knew more about ships and their routine than the Army, so in the long run we were able to get the best out of most of the deals, although most seemed to start heavily weighted in favour of the Army.

Steaming in a vast circle to keep out of range of enemy bombers meant that we were spending a fair amount of time sailing down the middle of the Atlantic – and it was November! We were almost constantly running into winter gales, and even those of us who were conditioned to the motion of small ships found the lazy antics of this 'old lady' a bit of a trial and once again had to find our sea-legs.

Below decks, and there seemed to be acres of it compared with the minesweepers, hundreds of very sorry men lay where ever space permitted; every messdeck table was littered with suffering humanity and, as each meal was missed, the more painful their condition became.

This was something that no amount of discipline could counter. The disorder on deck and below confounded all the hallowed routines and disciplines laid down by the Army. Men, hundreds of them, just did not care, all they wanted to do was to be left in peace – to die! Even those of us with naval-type stomachs finally succumbed to the stench and squalor.

As we moved south, the gales died down and we sailed into warmer and calmer waters. The recovery from what had seemed imminent death by the masses was dramatic. Once again the messdecks were scrubbed clean, clothes were washed and the queues to play 'housey housey' and, in quiet corners, the forbidden 'crown and anchor' reappeared.

Southwards, and the sun began to cast a different light on all our problems. The endless stews that had been served up in the Atlantic continued to appear in the tropics and, as filling as this food was it must be remembered that there were 8,000 mouths to feed most of them in their late teens or early twenties; with six sittings to each meal, which meant that as soon as one meal was finished men left the dining area and immediately joined the queue for the next – they were always ready to eat.

Apart from meals, endless queues formed at the ships NAAFI, at the barber's and at the library. Add to this one or two runs of lifeboat drill and it is easy to see that there was no privacy anywhere at any time.

Life, now that we were able to enjoy the warm sunshine, was boring at best, but the days passed and it was amazing how we all became resigned to the situation. The ocean now seemed empty except for our convoy, just thousands of square miles of nothingness. However, we awoke one morning to find that during the night we had been joined by one of our 'R'-class battleships, with attendant destroyers, and they stayed with us until we broke away to steam into Freetown, on the west coast of Africa, where we were to replenish our coal bunkers.

After weeks at sea in miserable living conditions the breathtaking first view of Freetown was something out of a picture-book – so green and lush. And there to sweep us into this 'white man's grave' of a port was my old ship, *Syringa*.

She survived the war working out of Freetown, but this was the last time I was to see her. I later learnt that shortly after I left her she steamed to Belfast for a long refit prior to this foreign draft; her mizzen had been taken out and a very workmanlike pair of point five, twin-barrelled guns fitted to the top of the galley. She had always sat smartly in the water, but now she looked even better.

How I wished I could have gone aboard, or even sent a signal to my old shipmates, and talked of the old times, of runs ashore in Grimsby, Hartlepool and Pompey, of the time we towed empty lifeboats into port from torpedoed freighters, or of the refugees after Dunkirk, in open boats and some even in canoes, streaming across the Channel. Or of the night we challenged a ship near the enemy coast and, on getting no reply, put a four-inch shell across her bow – and in firing cut away our own forestay. What a panic!

We would have talked of the dead picked-up and buried at sea, of being shelled from the French coast, and not liking it one little bit. How we could have 'swung the lamp' for old time's sake. But it was not to be; there was no way that I could get a signal to her.

For the next five days they bunkered ship laboriously, with little black men running up planks with rush baskets full of coal on their heads to tip into the side pocket bunker. There were droves of them, working endlessly, day and night, like a column of ants, singing and making great fun of their labour, until each man's grain of coal had multiplied into thousands of tons and we were full.

In the meantime, thousands of very green servicemen were obliged to look longingly at the lush vegetation on the not-so-far-away shore, without the slightest hope of being allowed to walk among it. Only in our dreams could we wander from this rustbucket, away across the calm water and into the palms and coloured vegetation, which all looked so cool. Its fruits were brought off daily to us in the dozens of 'bum' boats laden with oranges, limes, paw paws, coconuts and bananas. All had to be bartered for with the occupant of the boat – a new experience in itself.

They were very adept in throwing up to the prospective shopper a weighted line, attached to the other end of which was a shallow basket into which twelve oranges would be counted; a tight hold was kept on the basket until the transaction was completed. No amount of haggling would increase this twelve-for-a-shilling bargain, until 'One for the King' was shouted down, inferring that the thirteenth orange would be taken home to the King. Immediately, an extra orange was added to the basket and it could then be hauled up.

All this was done on complete trust that the shopper would return the shilling in the basket to the canoe below. Perhaps we were being overcharged on local values, but fresh fruit, after weeks in a troopship, was very welcome. Not all shoppers returned the shilling, just to hear how fluently these natives could curse, in every dialect known in the British Isles. They were particularly good at the Scottish.

Some were great swimmers and divers; they came aboard and, from the top bridge, which was at least eighty feet above the water, would dive in to retrieve the smallest coin flicked into the water.

All these new sights and sounds came to us thousands of miles from the war, blackouts and the Blitz, from rations and urgency. It all seemed so unreal to be here, on the west coast of Africa, in bright sunshine, massed together like cattle, eating oranges, paw paws, etc.; yet we knew that a massive convoy like this would be at its most vulnerable as soon as we moved out of this natural harbour, a perfect place for U-boats to home in on.

Among the many notices that adorned the messdecks was a warning not to buy any pets from the natives, but being the soft touch that he is the British serviceman was a pushover and after we had been at sea for some days a whole clutch of tropical birds turned up, and of all things a grown baboon had 'found' its way aboard – and no one knew how.

By this time the heat of the messdeck and the confined space had turned the animal quite nasty and it had to be shot. This was our first taste of a foreign port; no wonder the authorities gave us no shore leave – heaven knows what would have found its way aboard if they had.

With the last ship of the convoy bunkered, it was time to head out and steam south, into a brilliant tropical sunset, and once more we settled down to our animal-like existence aboard HM troopship *Empress of Asia*.

The days passed and the 'buzz' that we all wanted to believe was that the ship would bunker again at Cape Town. These rumours, as always, come straight from the galley. As we steamed on day after day, well out of sight of land, they became a flood, until the more experienced of us noted that our course was no longer south but eastwards. This, and the Cape Agullus roll, indicated that we had rounded the Cape and therefore would not be bunkering in Cape Town.

Next, our messdeck lawyers came up with the information that our next port of call must be Durban, for beyond that was the Indian Ocean, and in no way did we have enough bunker to cross that amount of ocean – and this time they were right, Durban it was.

In some respects, Weymouth harbour is a miniature of Durban, the Nothe becoming the Bluff, with a fine beach away to the right as you enter; the entrance is narrow and, like Weymouth, protected by a pier on the port hand for the great liners and ships of war that enter the run through the narrows, a 'hairy' experience for any navigator.

Within the narrow entrance, however, a vast harbour develops, big enough to take the entire convoy alongside. As we passed through the narrows there, far below us, was the figure of a woman, dressed all in white, with a large, red picture hat, singing each ship into this wonderful port with popular songs of the day. She became known to the many thousands of servicemen that passed through Durban as 'The Lady in White.'

To the men who came to Durban, this is still known as a paradise port, and the next three days were just that. Whatever mistakes South Africa has made in her internal affairs since the war, she made no mistakes in the way she entertained our servicemen then. It was just fantastic!'

Imagine many thousands of troops being let ashore after six weeks in the quite appalling conditions of troopship life – sailors, soldiers and airmen, masses of them, all now dressed in their best 'rig of the day,' surging out of the dock gates to be met by hordes of local people, all anxious to entertain them for the rest of the day and, if that were not enough, to do it again the next day, too.

We were taken to their homes, to sample food the like of which we had never tasted before: fruit of every kind, and as much as could be eaten. Nothing was too much trouble – we were treated as one of the family.

So pro-British were they that it mattered not if our money ran out. We could go ashore flat broke and come back replete in every way, with five quid in our pocket, stuffed into our shirt by some well-wisher from the 'old country'.

A large hall had been set aside called the 'Victoria Club.' Here, for only a token sum we were supplied with the most memorable 'big eats' of all time; after those weeks in a troopship, who could blame us if we went a little over the top, particularly with the fruit, which was plentiful and free.

It was great fun to be transported along West Street in a rickshaw drawn by an enormous Zulu in full tribal dress. We shopped for presents to send home and quite often were not allowed to pay for them – they even paid for the postage home! And, while buying in the larger stores, it was not unknown for the sales girl to invite you home. Paradise was not a good enough name for Durban, servicemen just could not go wrong there.

Of course it had to end. Our naval draft was duly ordered to pack and disembark. We had entertained hopes of spending the rest of the war in this heaven, but it was not to be.

We re-embarked into the British India boat *Aronda* and moved out of the harbour, turning northwards around the corner of South Africa.

After these few days in paradise it was not surprising to find that a few of our draft had gone AWOL in Durban, the temptations to remain in this 'heaven' proving more that some could resist.

Having now turned the southern tip of Africa and pointing northwards, we felt ourselves to be seasoned voyagers. No longer did the brilliant tropical sunsets fascinate us, and flying fish became commonplace. We had found ways of dodging the daily boat drills and some had found a way of beating the 'crown and anchor' boards. Once again we were nearing the Equator.

It was now obvious that we were destined for the Mediterranean, where the Navy's losses had been severe, a state of affairs which, as far as could be seen, was destined to continue. Our next anxiety was the type of ship we might get drafted to and, of even more importance, what sort of a CO we might get.

Our next landfall was Cape Guardafui, abeam to port, where we altered course for Aden, an arid desert of a port. There we unshipped some army personnel. Then on up the thousand miles of the Red Sea, a thousand miles of nothing on either side but more desert; the sunsets were fantastic but the heat of the day fast became unbearable.

Anchoring in the Gulf of Suez, the mammoth task of cleaning up the messdecks began. Everything had to be re-stowed in its right place; then the disembarkation of the many thousands of men began, all in the kind of heat to which we were not yet accustomed.

Away now by train, (or was it cattle trucks?) to Alexandria, a journey of some hours crossing a desert in the discomfort of a typical Egyptian train – slatted seats and window covered only by rattan blinds, through which blew the ubiquitous sand and cinders from the toiling engine. From later experience it was learnt that, whatever train we took, at whatever time of the day or night, from now on in Egypt we always managed to stop at a junction called Ben Ha – always to be pestered by hordes of shoeshine boys and even smaller boys selling 'eggs a bread.'

Our first hot and sticky night was spent at a shore base called HMS *Canopus*, where for the next few days we awaited our appointments to individual ships.

Canopus had seen a great deal of the war. Many of its ships' companies had been lost; we were their replacements.

My draft was not long in coming and it was to HMS *Cocker*. I joined her when she was in dry dock out at Gabarry. My first shock came when I saw that she was a converted Antarctic whaler, and underwater she was built to the shape of an egg, with no centre keel with which to grip the water, and no rolling chocks; so I had a fair idea from the very start that in heavy weather this was going to be a swine to live in.

I was to relieve an RN chief coxswain, a time-serving man who knew all the tricks of the trade – and was good enough to pass some on to me.

He frightened the hell out of me by taking me on the bridge to explain my duties and warning me darkly how tender she was on the helm and how careful I must be.

Here it should be explained, that the purpose, in the working life of this class of ship was to be so manoeuvrable at answering the helm that the bloody job of exterminating whales could be ruthlessly carried out. This made them highly efficient at their job, but skittish and volatile.

In their newly acquired job of hunting U-boats, these converted whalers had proved to be equally efficient at sea in heavy weather and under helm. They would bury themselves in the seas but still shake themselves free. The great flare of the bows testified to this quality, and sweeping aft to no more than eighteen inches of freeboard made what would have been on a normal deck, an impossible passage.

Nevertheless she was manoeuvrable and could spin on a six-pence, and when we rang down for full speed ahead from an engine capable of producing 2,800 horse-power in a 300-ton ship she virtually leapt forward.

HMS *Cocker*, like all her sister ships, and there had been twenty-one of them, had begun life as a 'Kos' boat; before being renamed *Cocker*, she had been *Kos 19*. These ships had proved to be a welcome addition to the Fleet when its losses had been severe enough for the authorities to scour the world for likely vessels to fill the gaps in our defence. In the Med they had won for themselves the name of 'maids of all work'.

It was in fact from these whalers that our bigger corvettes were designed and evolved. We became known for our versatility, chasing up stragglers, guarding cripples, standing by the broken ones, picking up survivors, towing, escorting – we had great power for our size.

We carried some twenty depth-charges and bristled with small-calibre guns, some won from our various visits to Tobruk, from stacks of equipment left by the retreating Italians. Our favourite was an adapted anti-tank gun called the Isotti, which had about an inch calibre.

As the losses of the Fleet destroyers had risen from the many engagements around the Med; these small craft were put in to fill the sad gaps and carried loads far in excess of their size.

So, we went to war doing the job of a corvette, working with the big boys and, to begin with a crew that had yet to be shaken down.

Nothing achieves this faster than action, and this was not long in coming. The great and most welcome change was that to oil fuel – no more of the accursed coal, we could come in from sea, make fast alongside the oiler, pipe 'All hands to breakfast' and, by the time the meal was cleared away, we were bunkered, and ready to uncouple and move to No. 42 shed for storing. By 1400, hands could be going ashore.

Having listened to the outgoing coxswain, I took the helm for the first time with great trepidation. His last words of warning to me were. 'Be very careful with the amount of helm you use, don't use too much. Take the wheel from five to port to five to starboard and you'll roll all the crockery off the table.'

He wasn't joking, either. Later, much later, when even a coxswain had reason to brood over the way he thought he had been treated, he could, by taking a bit of unnecessary avoiding action, tip the officers' coffee into their laps while they were having their meal.

No one wandered on the deck of that ship. She was strong and robust, quick and tender. If ever there was a ship that needed a net over the funnel in bad weather to keep the stokers in – this was the one.

Chapter Eight

A Whale-Chaser to Chase the U-boats

As I lay flat on my back in my bunk right down aft, over the propellor shaft, she could, and did, fling me out time after time. How we cursed her, but how we thrilled as she came about at full speed and tore off on a U-boat chase with the big boys.

Soon the whole crew had shaken down into an efficient unit, especially the depth-charge crew, for they had the added discomfort of having to do their work of re-loading on a rolling deck constantly awash with great seas.

In the weeks that followed, we convoyed, we chased, we chivvied, we put men aboard flaming tankers, we bandaged the wounded, we pitied the ones who were burnt – even wished they would die, for there was so little we could do for them. We experienced the stench of burnt flesh, the gore of mangled limbs and bodies. We saw gallantry 'beyond the call of duty', as the book says.

We helped take many brave convoys out of Alexandria *en route* to Tobruk. How brave we looked, only to be torn apart before the first twenty-four hours had passed. So full at times were we with survivors picked up from the sea that we had to be re-routed back to Alexandria to discharge our human cargo and leave again to rejoin the convoy.

Our title of 'maid of all work' was not easily won. There were many times when we could not fight the ship, because of the number of survivors we had picked up. They lay in the alleyways, around the funnel, in the galley, and anywhere on the upper deck. We wiped the oil fuel from their mouths and their eyes, we cleaned up their vomit and what clothes we had we gave them.

Those who could eat, ate all we had. We saw them die! Many died quietly in a corner, far, far from home and family, their creased and broken bodies now an insult to the manhood they used proudly to possess.

The badly burnt ones I learnt to detest; they haunted me in my sleep – and still do at times. They cried out in their agony – and there was so little that we could do for them.

Some cursed to the very end; others, who realised that there was little we could do for them, asked us to do what we could for the less injured. They were the quiet ones, quiet at their work, not boasting as some do to boost their ego; in their quiet moments they had arranged their thoughts for just such an occasion as this, and they sat and smoked until we found them dead.

What did all these experiences leave us with? Pity? I cannot remember pity, just a lasting contempt for war and all its waste, but above all the memory of the men who had died well, for I suspect that they had also lived well.

We continued to run the gauntlet to Tobruk for many months. Our greatest dread was the 'Stuka'. These planes attacked by coming right down the funnel and the one great bomb that they carried was all for you. To add to its terror the enemy fixed screamers to the wings of the plane; the nerve-jangling noise that these made in their dive could never be forgotten.

It took men of steel to hold their fire until a stuka had pulled out of its dive; then, with their soft underbelly exposed, our Isotti gun could score on a very vulnerable target.

At last the authorities heeded the view that the only way to effectively fight off this sort of attack was to arm all ships with enough small-arms automatic weapons so that everyone on deck could grab a machine-gun and spray up a sort of hose-pipe of bullets. If this could be carried out by a dozen or so ratings this would be effective – and it was.

From this idea a story worth the telling. Hung at any convenient place around the upper deck we had an assortment of machine-guns. One in particular was a 'strip Lewis'. It had no kick, tended to jump *away* from the shoulder and so had to be rigidly controlled, otherwise it would take charge.

In one particular attack our cook, a smallish chap, grabbed this gun and belted away, but the gun had predictably taken charge and he sprayed the upper deck, in the process shooting through one of the ship's boat-falls.

Unfortunately, feeling guilty, he said nothing to anyone. Had he done so it would have been a simple matter to renew the damaged rope, but it remained unnoticed until some days later, while we were at anchor in Tobruk harbour, where we received a signal from NOIC Tobruk requesting to see our CO in his office ashore.

'Away seaboats' crew' was piped and, due to the peculiar design of a whaler, which made entry into the boat difficult, it was lowered with its crew sat with oars tossed to the level where the CO stepped into the boat.

Unfortunately, his weight was the straw that broke the camel's back. The falls parted and the boat's crew, with our commanding officer in his best No. 11's, were all dumped into the water. Oars and bottom boards went floating away and all the heavy gear sank, while crew and the CO struggled in the water. As the CO was hauled back aboard he 'invited' me to see him in his cabin in the morning!

He wasn't a very big chap, but he had my guts for garters – and the rest of the crew knew this; there's nothing that goes down so well in the fo'c'sle as their knowing that the coxswain had a 'bottle' from the old man – they loved it!

The end of this story came a few nights later while we were back at sea. It was dusk and after being relieved of the watch, I was aware of someone in the shadows, and said, 'Who is that?'

'It's the cook.'

'What are you doing on deck at this time, you are a daysman and should be in your hammock.'

'I can't sleep,' he said and then the whole story came out about shooting the boat-falls away.

It had obviously been on his mind ever since and knowing that I had taken what was really his medicine from the old man he had to own up. Poor little cookie was not to survive when we got the torpedo with our number on it. The coxswain's responsibilities are many and varied; among them is to see that all equipment is kept in running order, therefore the matter of the captain being dumped into the sea was down to me.

Many years later, after the war had ended, my wife and I toured Ireland and in Londonderry met my old CO again over a long, long lunch. I recounted how the boat-falls had been shot away. I also told him the full story of the pink panties at Haifa, but more of that later.

On this particular convoy to Tobruk we had set out from Alexandria and as soon as we had settled down and cleared the 'great pass' (the swept channel) and taken up our allocated station of 'arse-end charlie', we were attacked by Stukas.

The duty of the 'charlie' was to keep to the rear of the convoy, maintaining a good Asdic watch for 'U'-boats, which developed the habit of trailing the convoy and calling up other 'U'-boats as required.

A further duty, and a most distasteful one, was that of closing any torpedoed ship, with the hope of perhaps being able to tow her to safety or pick up survivors,

We began picking up survivors from the word go and the more we proceeded the more we had to pick up, until all our reserve blankets and a great deal of our personal clothing had been given away to the dozens of survivors now aboard. By the second day we had so many that we could not move about the ship, so we were ordered back to Alexandria as fast as possible. We steamed up Alex harbour looking, with all our survivors festooned about out decks, less like an HM ship than was usual.

'Rig of the day' for entering harbour was out of the question, for we had given most of our clothes away, besides, we were warmed by the feeling that we had just done a commendable job of rescue.

This was shattered by a signal from Admiral Vian's flagship, instructing our CO to appear 'forthwith' aboard his cruiser, and when the Navy says 'forthwith' it means *now*.

Dressed in his best No. 1 suit, our diminutive CO stood on the quarterdeck of the cruiser and was given the dressing-down of his life for having dared to bring one of HM ships into a harbour where the admiral was present without the crew being in the 'rig of the day'. The fact that we had been seeing to the comfort of so many survivors did not seem to matter.

Trip after trip to Tobruk was beginning to wear away our nerves, and so occasionally we were routed to Haifa or Port Said. The only intimation that the crew had of our destination was to stand on the upper deck and at the end of the 'great pass' turn to port if Tobruk or to starboard if it was Haifa. If it was to starboard, the crew were hilarious, for up there in Haifa there was little to see of the war and the kind Jewish ladies of that port ran a very fine servicemen's club where the 'big eats' were as unending as they were free.

We all used to dream of getting a run up to Haifa; it was nothing less than a rest period. Perhaps the powers-that-be knew this.

Painting ship on the way was no chore and a distinct air of it being fair day was apparent. Those who know this port will remember that it was the terminal for the overland pipeline from Iraq; consequently the jetty was enormously long, capable of taking two of the largest tankers of the day alongside.

On this occasion we had tied up at the far end from the town and, for some reason, there was a curfew operating. This meant that shore leave was piped from noon until 1600, a most unusual occurrence.

With leave-takers gone ashore, I settled down to a quiet afternoon 'make and mend' until 1600, at which time the quartermaster came along to my cabin with the leave book showing that AB Green was adrift.

Normally I should have gone straight to the officer of the watch and reported this. But Green was a reliable sort of chap who never to date had let me or the ship down, so, wrongly, I decided to give him a few more minutes, put the leave book in the rack, and promptly forgot all about it.

At 'Pipe down' I realised that not only was Green in trouble but so was I, for not reporting his absence to the OOW. I slept very little that night and as we were sailing at 0600 next morning I was up holding the baby for a man adrift.

The ship was astir now and there was still no sign of Green. We were singling up fore and aft and I was on the bridge testing all communications prior to the CO coming up to take her to sea. Within minutes the CO would have to be told. When way down this long jetty there appeared what looked like a naked figure. It was Green, and he was running for all he was worth, trying to get back aboard before we sailed.

He was, in fact, completely naked except for a pair of lady's pink panties. He came pounding aboard. If this could be accomplished without any of the officers seeing him, both he and I would have been let off the hook; the crew knew this and ushered him below. He changed smartly, as he was the Asdic rating of the watch, and, luckily for me, just before the CO entered the bridge to take the ship to sea Green was sat at his duty-station in full command of the situation.

The full story came out later in the day. Green had gone into the 'red light district' to partake of the fruits, and while he was performing his clothes were stolen, leaving him in a bit of a spot.

He knew that the curfew would shortly be coming into operation, so he decided to stay under cover and enjoy some more of the fruit, hoping that at dawn he could get back aboard, as in fact he managed to do, with the help of a pair of 'borrowed' pink panties.

Now, Green was a fine swimmer and a great-diver and ever after this when 'Hands to bathe and skylark' was piped he would appear in his pink panties, to the roars of the rest of the crew, and would make his way to the top bridge, from where he would make the most beautiful swallow-dive into the sea.

The officers knew that there must be a story behind all this but, to their credit, they never insisted on being told the truth.

Many years later, in Londonderry with the CO the full story was told. It was just as well for me that things went that way, for this was the same CO who was to recommend me to take a commission later on. Had he perhaps known all the facts at the time, he might never have given me the necessary recommendation to school for a commission, with this as well as the matter of the boat-falls down to me.

Much more running the gauntlet up into Tobruk had yet to be done and, in the late evening of one of those trips, we were attacked from the air and a quiet old freighter called 'Calderon' had her bow-plates blown in by a near-miss. She began to sink by the head and as usual we went alongside and started to take off the crew. This completed, we stood off, watching her slowly sink. Her cargo was cased petrol for the Army at Tobruk.

Suddenly the chief engineer of the Calderon came to the bridge and volunteered the information that he had left the engine-room without having switched off the dynamos; if as she sank they were to earth there would be sparks and, in this heavily laden, petrol-soaked air, she would blow up.

If we could put him back aboard and he could throw the switches and she did not sink, then we could tow her to Tobruk, and her valuable cargo would be saved.

With this in mind, and the thoughts of salvage looming large in the imagination of the crew, *Cocker* closed the wounded *Calderon*.

Upon reflection, it would seem that because we were close, close enough for the blast to pass over us, moving in was a prudent move. Suddenly, possibly because a bulkhead had collapsed, she sank quite quickly by the head, and then, in an instant blew up in one gigantic explosion probably caused by a spark from her dynamo. The heat was searing and, with most of our paintwork peeling off, we thanked our protecting gods that we were close enough for the blast to have missed us. We survived with just the loss of our eyebrows and a bit of paintwork.

They must have assumed in the convoy, which had kept plodding on, that we were lost, for no one could have escaped that fireball.

We rang 'full ahead' and made after the convoy as fast as we could, bearing the crew of the *Calderon* and a much-shaken chief engineer.

A wartime Admiralty publication contained the following:

> The little maids of all work were, however, the anti-submarine patrol vessels. Two of them, the *Kos 19* and the *Kos 21*, were under the command of Lieutenants J. Scott RNVR and A. R. J. Tilson RNR respectively. The *Kos 21* was one of the little ships that succeeded in struggling back from Crete. She was sunk in October while towing a 'D' lighter to Tobruk; although hit by a large armour-piercing bomb, there was only one casualty. The last, the *Kos 19*, was renamed 'Cocker'. There was no task, from submarine-hunting to escorting or towing, that these little ships did not undertake with cheerful competence.

The *Cocker* earned a letter of congratulations from the Commander-in-Chief for 'excellent seamanship on the part of the commanding officer and the ship's company'.

Then came the unexpected: we turned out of Alex and made our way to Port Said. There we waited under instructions until a very large freighter loaded with enormous gun-barrels and locomotives on her upper deck made ready for sea. While we did so we enjoyed the comparative peace of that port. Due to the lack of jetty space it was customary here to drop anchor and then go astern until quarterly lines could be made fast to the jetty. In this way many more vessels could take advantage of a small area: each ship was now within chatting distance of its neighbour.

During the days that followed, it was customary at noon every day for a great scow of a boat under two great sweep oars to come pulling back with a load of Egyptian workers from Worms Island, at the other side of the Canal. This scow was so heavily laden with humanity that there was scarcely a plank out of the water and each day as, they glided in between us and the next ship, our messdeck comedian stood waiting on the wing of the bridge and, as they passed abeam, he would offer two cigarettes to the natives and then throw them into the scow. Every day there would be the same scene, all this humanity lunging upwards to catch the fags, and every day the scow sank, and the men struggled ashore and bailed out the boat ready for the same event tomorrow, without the slightest rancour, it seemed.

Lying stern to this jetty for the first time, we were approached by what is locally known as 'gilly gilly men', who ask permission to come aboard during 'stand easy' or mealtimes to entertain the ship's company with their conjuring tricks. In the first instance all seems innocent and above-board until from experience it is learnt that, while the main body of the crew is being entertained, an accomplice has adroitly pushed the eye of a four inch rope overboard, so that another accomplice in a boat can come along, possibly after dark, and pull the rope down into his boat; thus is a valuable piece of vital equipment lost. These same men operated in the streets of the towns and cities – having collected a crowd of servicemen around them the entertainment was so totally absorbing that it was not until later that a paybook or two was found to be missing.

These entertainers, plus the beggars, lepers and vendors of leather handbags, dirty postcards and fruit, as well as the constant bevy of small boys offering the services of their smaller sisters, made a 'run ashore' seem like a walk in a minefield.

Chapter Nine

A Katabatic Storm

Then we sailed, with our single-funnelled freighter we turned to starboard out of Port Said, where at the end of a long sea-wall De Lesseps stood on his pedestal with hand outstretched, on up past our much-loved Haifa, right on up into the Gulf of Iskenderun to the Turkish port of Alexandretta. This being a neutral port while we were a ship of war we had to wait outside their twelve-mile limit until our freighter had discharged her cargo. As this consisted of very heavy single goods, it was to take a few days, and in the meantime we painted ship.

At the end of each day's work, we piped 'all hands to bathe and skylark'. On the second day, with most of the crew in the water, we were fired on by the Turkish shore batteries – great eight-inch bricks. Although they fell well short they served as a reminder that we had drifted inside their territorial waters. We were out of the water quicker than that and ringing down for 'full ahead' to get out of the danger zone.

We all took a dim view of that, especially as we had just convoyed badly needed goods to a so-called 'friendly' neutral.

So we welcomed the sight of our now unloaded freighter coming out of Alexandretta, took station abeam and set course for home waters.

En route one of the katabatic storms that this part of the eastern Mediterranean is known for hit us. It seemed to come out of nowhere. The 'glass' had shown no signs or warning of its approach and so we had had little time to prepare ourselves to meet what was coming. In its intensity, this storm beat anything that I had experienced; even the North Atlantic storms had nothing on this one. It was vicious!

It was dark even at noon and the enormously deep seas which were whipped up in a very short time gave us the hammering of our life. She buried herself continually and all we could do was to put her head to sea and plod on at just steerage way. The spume swept from the tops of the waves kept us in a continual mist, so that visibility from the wheelhouse was nil.

The man who designed these ships should have designed the men to go with them, for she flung us all over the place until our bodies were black with bruises, our legs ached and our heads reeled. No one was safe on deck but, as always at times like these, something, somewhere not stowed correctly will break free and seamen have to risk life and limb to get it lashed and stowed again.

Swamped as she was, she could always shake herself free of the great weight of water that surged over us, staggering and plunging, yawing and corkscrewing, vibrating enough to shake one's teeth out when the propeller came out of the water, and as it bit again into the water the jarring effect on the main engines could be felt through the deck.

Luckily for me, I was on watch when this storm hit us, for in no time at all it became clear that those of us on the bridge would not be getting off, and those off watch would have to remain battened down in the messdeck until these great seas no longer surged over us.

We spent some eight hours on the bridge that day, without any hot food or drink, wedged as best we could in any convenient corner and each taking turns at the wheel to relieve the tedium and strain.

We seemed to be more of a submarine than a surface vessel, with at times only our upper structure and part of the forrard gun sticking out of the solid water. It seemed that we could never free ourselves from this terrible weight of seething water, which seemed to leap at us in great pyramids from all sides, in such fury that we must be overwhelmed.

But at her work in the Southern Ocean, the *Cocker* had seen this, and worse, many time before. She seemed to know instinctively just what to do to shake herself free. In spite of all our anxieties, it seems in retrospect that she was in her element; it was only we, the men, who were not.

However, as always the storm passed and the sun came out, and I remembered the text in the wheelhouse of '*Syringa*' – 'He who sends the storm guides the ship'. We could have done with Him in the wheelhouse!

It was not surprising, after many hours of nil visibility, that when at last we had a chance to look around we had lost our freighter – but in its place was a quite different one – with a large cinder guard on the top of its funnel!

Who was going to tell the 'Old Man' this? I could imagine the leg-pull in the officers' club about the ship that got away. Of course he had to be told and this resulted in all the officers being called to the bridge for a conference. I seem to remember that this relieved me to go and make a comprehensive list of all the damage sustained – bent stanchions, broken boats, smashed crockery, all our fresh vegetables ruined, wardroom and messdecks awash. But with all the proper forms duly made out, replacements were provided when we got back to base.

Going down into the messdeck to see the state of affairs there, a sight I shall never forget met my eyes. In this class of ship the messdeck was about the size of a normal lounge. A companionway led from the deckhand to the deck; on each side of this was a messdeck table running fore and aft, with long forms on which to sit to table. An old-fashioned combustion stove stood centrally at the foot of the companionway.

Individual lockers lined the side of the ship and if you were a long-standing member of the crew you owned one; otherwise you lived out of your kitbag. Hammock hooks were welded to the deckhead and, again, if you were a senior you got a hammock space, which you guarded jealously.

If you were a 'sprog', you found a space to sleep either on a messdeck table or on a lounge stool. In this confined space some twenty men lived, ate, argued, slept, wrote their letters, did their ironing, darned their socks and played cards.

The scene that I met was total devastation! Four inches of water sloshed from side to side as she rolled; lockers had been torn from the ship's side and lay open with the contents spewed out all over the deck.

Seaboots, woollen scarves, writing-paper, all raced from side to side, oilskins and a duffle coat or two clogged the hammock netting; and, to cap it all, the last meal attempted was half a dozen tins of 'herrings in tomato sauce'. All had been emptied into a large flat baking-tin and had been left unattended for only a second. The result of this moment of inattention was that the whole of this squalid mess was now a technicolour mess surging around with all the rest of the debris.

To this day, I can still smell the result of this frightful concoction and wonder how it was that from this mess men could pick themselves up and only an hour or so after regaining calmer waters have it all tidied up and shipshape once again.

These 'whale-catchers' were Norwegian, and quite unlike any other ship afloat. They were perfected for the purpose of hunting and killing whales, following the invention and development of a suitable gun. They were small, sturdy vessels of around 300 tons but with a capacity of engine for towing far in excess of anything else their size. Highly flared bows with a great deal of sheer, and a very low freeboard, made them easily recognisable. They had rounded bottoms, to facilitate rapid manoeuvrability; this feature, however, made them roll like a barrel and they would pitch and perform all manner of inexplicable gyrations, so as to defy description.

The only thing they almost never did was sink, although quite often they technically foundered (this means plunging below the surface). Several had been known to turn turtle, but always finished up righting themselves. 'These were not ships for the faint-hearted or those of delicate stomachs, for in what would be called calm weather they would dance about perpetually.' (From 'Follow the Whale' by Ivan Sanderson, 1958). We used to say of them that they would dance about on damp grass.

One of our stoker POs had, in the depression of the 1930s on the Tyne, signed on as a stoker for a season in a Norwegian Antarctic whaling expedition and expected to be away down in the Southern Ocean for about three months. He served down there in a catcher of the same class as 'Cocker' and it was through him that we were made aware of the sea-keeping antics of this type of vessel. We thought at times that he was inclined to exaggerate, but now we had the cuts and bruises to prove all his claims, and that far-fetched story, told me now so long ago, of the need to put a net over the top of the funnel to catch the stokers seemed to have some relevance after all.

At the end of the catching season, in order to earn more money for his family at home, he had volunteered to 'over winter' in South Georgia, carrying out the necessary maintenance to the catcher fleet for the following season. 'Never again,' he used to say. 'Seven months entirely cut off from civilisation, in the bitterest of weather, winds of hurricane force that never seemed to end, blinding snow storms and precious little daylight – never again'.

This stint carried straight on into the next whaling season, at the end of which, flushed with money – from nine months' earnings, for there was little to spend money on in South Georgia, although had they been paid by the hours put in they would have been poorly paid – he, like many others, took passage in the mother ship 'Balaena' back to Durban for onward passage back to the Tyne and the big payoff.

So who was to blame him if he 'subbed' some money and had a run ashore at Durban? This must have been a monumental binge, for he woke up penniless on the beach, only to learn that the 'Balaena' had sailed without him.

He now had no option but to scratch a living as a beachcomber until the 'Balaena' returned the next year for a further season 'down South', for this was the only way that he could get back to his wife and family on the Tyne. So he had to spend two catching seasons and one 'over winter' away – in all some fifteen months.

He finally returned home with just about nine weeks' catching pay in his pocket, less the cost of having to buy a further kit of winter clothes from the slop chest. All this he had endured in order to get away from the Depression on the Tyne and, hopefully, to provide something better for his family . . . Some character was George the Geordie, and a great shipmate; as small as he was, he was frightened of nothing on two legs and not so much on four.

Many of these crewmen, like myself, had only a handful of time before been pampered by an over-indulgent mother, our every wish-had-been attended to. A drawer only had to be opened and there in neat stacks were well-darned socks, a pile of handkerchiefs, shirts and underclothes. We hadn't given a thought to how much care and work had gone into all these items appearing in their appointed places. The value of the space that we lived in at home and the privacy that it allowed us was now sorely missed; here in a small ship, living cheek-by-jowl with a score or so of other men was a numbing experience.

Some of the men were loud-mouthed, coarse and belligerent, talking with accents so foreign to our own ears. Others in our mind's eyes, we had put into the same category as ourselves as far as background was concerned, and we had unwittingly gravitated towards them.

Then again, there was a sprinkling of well-mannered chaps, 'out of the top drawer' – they talked of Plato and Shakespeare and were articulate in so many subjects. Mostly they had had a public-school education and they had not found it so difficult to adjust to this dormitory-like existence as I had, for they had left the doting care of a mother when they were about ten years old or less and had been well accustomed to having to fend for themselves in the spartan life that was said to be the lot of a public-school boy.

My adjustment to these harsh conditions had been more difficult and the total lack of privacy had baffled me; trying to live out of a kitbag for weeks on end had appalled me, and even the language used in normal conversation had stunned me.

But in their wisdom – or perhaps they had no other solution to the problem – the Admiralty had pitch forked this strange assortment of men into the messdecks of all its ships, big or small, and it was surprising how, in a very short space of time, there emerged from this melêe a ship's company.

A ship's company so proud of their ship that, at the drop of a hat when ashore, they would literally fight for the honour of that ship, were its name besmirched.

I had served my apprenticeship in messdecks peopled by men from Poland, Labrador, New Zealand, South Africa, Wales, Scotland, and an even more contentious mixture of men from the various counties of England.

What an impossible mixture! But it worked.

As a consolation prize, and to get the ship cleaned up, we were ordered into Haifa, where once we had refuelled and the ship been considered clean, shore leave was piped and all the vicissitudes of the recent storm were washed aft and forgotten – at least for the few hours we spent ashore.

I remembered thinking when I got my draft to the Mediterranean that any fool could be a sailor out there – blue skies, summer all year round, no fog to plague a sailor's life – good ho! – but here we were licking our wounds, having survived what later I realised was undoubtedly the worst storm in the whole of my wartime service.

As for the fact that we had lost our charge, the freighter, the wardroom kept very tight-lipped about the result of a minor enquiry that took place. We had, in fact, escorted a ship back, if not the one that we had set out with; perhaps losing one but finding another cancelled each other out!

Chapter Ten

The Death of 'Cocker'

The loss of warships in the Mediterranean in general, and in Crete, Malta and Tobruk in particular, had sapped the destroyer strength of the Fleet, leaving serious gaps, gaps that had to be filled. The search for likely vessels to fill these gaps led to the Antarctic, where a flotilla of whale-catchers was found and requisitioned.

It was, in fact, from these vessels that the basic design for the wartime corvette was adapted. The latter had developed into ships of around 800 tons, while whale-catchers only tipped the scales at 300 tons; but nevertheless, in the role of escort and convoy, they filled the gaps left by 1,200-ton destroyers.

Anything less like a British warship it would be hard to imagine than HMS *Cocker*. She lay in Tobruk harbour, *Cocker* an unlikely ship in unnatural waters, far, far from home. Even her saucy name was unreal, for she had been launched in the 1930s as the more prosaic *Kos 19* and had served her peacetime masters well down south, in the most relentless of oceans, doing the toughest and bloodiest of jobs, killing the Great Blue Whale.

Now here she was, on this June day in 1942, lolling in warm waters, renamed and fitted out with all the paraphernalia of war, guns, Asdic and depth-charges. Requisitioned only a year before, *Cocker*, like others of her kind, had been brought up from the bottom of the world for service in the Royal Navy as an anti-submarine vessel in the Mediterranean.

Call her what you will, try to hide her under Admiralty grey paint, dress her crew in the 'rig of the day', still at sea, doing a punishing fourteen knots, with her midship deck awash, she was an ugly duckling. In her brief year of war so far she had been a 'maid of all work', escorting, towing and 'arse-end Charlie-ing', and she had earned several commendations.

Now, due to the sad losses, she was sharing the work of escorting supply ships along the northern coast of Africa, from Alexandria to Tobruk and back.

On this occasion, as on many previously, *Cocker* slipped out of Tobruk harbour just before dark to carry out the necessary Asdic sweep of the harbour approaches prior to the arrival of a single-funnelled freighter, '*Hanna Moller*'. Once she appeared, *Cocker* and her infinitely more imposing companion ship, the naval corvette HMS *Gloxinia* – nearly three times as big – would take up station and, as fast as the freighter's tired old engines would allow, they would steam down to Alexandria and there enjoy the 'big eats' at the Fleet Club that all naval crews dream about when they are at sea.

On this occasion, however, there were snags. The wayward freighter did not appear at the appointed time, so *Cocker* swept and re-swept, probing with her Asdic finger for any sign of the underwater enemy, whose habit it was to sit quietly outside harbours for just such situations as this.

The crew, still at 'leaving harbour' stations, began to get irritable when the CO showed no sign of setting the watch, which would have allowed the bulk of the men to go below.

It was quite dark. Tiring of the constant pressure and the danger of crossing and re-crossing courses with our big sister in the blackness, we lay to and carried out a 360-degree sweep. The air was like velvet, the ship blacked out, yet all were aware of the urgency.

Didn't this crazy merchantman realise that by dawn we should be well beyond the German dive-bomber range?

Apparently not! We cursed her, the 'slab-sided bastard', for the longer we waited for her to appear, the more likely we were to have Stukas with our breakfast.

Then: 'Captain, Sir – vessel passing through the boom.' A sharp command, our telegraphs to the engine-room jangled, and we leapt to life. Much to our surprise, we took up station on the freighter's port quarter – her seaward side. Our more usual – and, it was thought, safer side – was the shore side when escorting so large a ship, a position which, as the voyage progressed, took us comfortably along under the cliffs. But, this station had been pinched by 'Gloxinia' pushing us out into the fully exposed seaward side of this miniature convoy.

At last the port watch was set, and the comforting vibrations of our engines, at a modest 'seven O' revolutions, were taking us back to our home base.

I was relieved at midnight. Savouring the now cool air, I went aft, where, following instructions that all off-watch personnel must sleep on deck whilst in this danger area, I had brought my camp-bed up from below.

Having first prepared my bed, I stood eating a doorstep of a third-grade salmon sandwich, which I had made from the leftovers of our last meal, before getting my head down to the pure bliss of, at the most, three hours' sleep.

The jangling alarm-bells jerked me back to life! As if driven by some monumental sledgehammer, an enemy torpedo rammed itself into the very vitals of Cocker! Instantly our ship and home was no longer either. She seemed to disintegrate, almost dissolve, into the sea.

A second explosion followed, probably the boilers going up, and by the light of flickering flames it was obvious that she had been blown in two, collapsing her at about midship-point into a mass of rending metal.

The stern, still motivated by the revolving propeller, seemed now to be crushing forwards and downwards onto the rapidly sinking bow section. There were noises – grinding metal, rushing water and steam rushing out of fractured pipes, bulkheads collapsing – and the agonised cries of trapped shipmates.

The stern began to rise clear of the water and as it did so the activating arm of the ship's whistle on the funnel dropped forward and there began a long, drawn-out wail until she died.

I clambered up the canting deck to the stern rail, and climbed over the rail onto what would normally be the vertical plates of the transome, now nearly horizontal.

There, to my horror, I saw the propeller still furiously turning at 'seven O' revolutions – so that was what seventy revolutions looked like!

My racing thoughts were now playing tricks; in the midst of all this chaos and din, I recalled in absolute detail the day when, as a boy, wilfully playing in a friend's farmyard with a chaff-cutting machine, I had accidentally cut the top off of another boy's thumb. I wondered if I was now to be chaff for these great revolving blades.

Although I had seen similar disasters overtake a dozen or so other ships, I could not believe that this had actually happened to us. But the noise was real and so was the flotsam now swirling past – men in the water gasping with the shock of immersion in water and crude oil. My brain cleared, I only had seconds to get away, not only from the propeller blades but from the sinking depth-charges. We carried some twenty in the racks and at least two would have been primed and ready, which meant that, when the mangled ship had sunk to the required depth, the whole lot would blow up.

In a frenzy I stripped off all my top gear, but a navy-blue rollnecked pullover, recently arrived from home, defied all my efforts to get it over my head.

Nor could I swim a yard with it on. There was nothing for it but to cut it off, which I did blessing the fact that I had a jackknife on a lanyard around my middle and wondering at the same time just what my sister would have said at seeing her knitted labour of love being cut to ribbons. Then I swam as far as I could to get away from the suction of the ship and the slowly sinking depth-charges.

It was scarcely minutes since the torpedo had struck, but it seemed like a lifetime. In the dark I could hear men talking in the sea quite close to me. I eased my swimming pace and looked back at the remains of the ship, now bolt upright in the water, with the propeller still flapping round. She began to slide, accompanied by the never-to-be-forgotten death sounds of a ship broken and doomed.

Bulkheads were crashing, great bubbles of air came vomiting up to the surface and the nudity of those parts of a ship normally only seen when in dry dock was as starkly shocking as one's first view of female nudity. Above all this cacophony of sound, I heard a voice call out in agony, 'I can't swim! I can't swim' . . . and a quite callous and matter-of-fact voice from another direction answered, 'You've left it bloody late to learn, chum.'

Cocker vanished in a welter of volcanic eruptions, leaving a sudden and heavy silence, and for those of us left in the sea began the soul-destroying task of finding out who of the ship's company was left.

The crude oil was warm and smooth to the touch, but it tasted vile – choking coughs in the darkness began to indicate the presence of survivors. There seemed at first to be a fair number of us in the water, but sound at sea-level can be deceptive. Calls of men to their mates and the shouts of others telling of what wreckage they were hanging on to confused the air; it seemed that the best there was on offer was half a Carley float.

Then we became aware of the thud of approaching propellers and pent-up feelings gave way to rousing cheers. It seemed as if half the ship's company had survived and were now intent on making themselves heard.

But our shouts and cheers died miserably away as it slowly began to register that the approaching vessel was, with regret, carrying out the newest Fleet Order – that the enemy must be sought out and destroyed, regardless of survivors.

We were now consumed with a slow build-up of hatred for the men in the fast-approaching corvette, who in seconds now would be hurling depth-charges among us. Yet, as bitter as we felt, we knew that the captain was only carrying out instructions, for it had been found from experience that enemy 'U'-boats, having torpedoed a ship, would not make haste *away* from the sinking vessel, but would close the wreck and sink with it, thereby hoping to avoid detection from our Asdics.

'Gloxinia' came hounding on at a great pace, and as more men in the water realised what was about to happen, great oaths were hurled at the ship, which only half an hour before we had chatted with by the Aldis lamp.

'Swim away! Get out! My brain told me, and, naked except for a pair of khaki shorts, I struck out as fast as I was able. Here fate took a hand, as from close by a panic-stricken cry for help came from a young seaman, all tangled up with what he thought to be an undersea monster.

I stopped swimming to help him, but it turned out that his trouser belt had broken, allowing his trousers to slip down around his legs and thus hamper his movements. By good luck we came across a Dan buoy (a small, flagged buoy) spewed out of the wreckage and I hoisted him up onto this, quickly following him, and got the buoy under our stomachs with our legs still dangling in the water.

We had just made it when 'Glaxinia' fired, dropping a pattern of depth-charges. The seconds that followed these charges as they sank to the required depth to explode seemed like weeks, for we knew that what was to follow would be eruptions the like of which we had seen many times before, but this time we would be on the receiving end.

Mule-like kicks hit me in the tail-bone, travelled up my spine and clamoured to get out of my skull. It was sheer hell – but being halfway out of the water we were relieved of the full force of the explosion and so survived, while others around us died horribly.

Afterwards it went strangely quite, no chattering voices or calling to shipmates; it seemed that each of us still alive was now afraid to call out in case he should find himself to be the lone survivor from this assault.

Gradually Cocker's survivors did come together. There were fewer than a dozen of us, including the commanding officer (Lieut. John Scott RNVR). His escape had been the narrowest. He was in his cabin, dazed and going down with his ship, when he heard quick voices above saying, 'The Old Man is dead, he must be' which roused him. He managed to slither out through a porthole, which had only been enlarged three months before for just such an emergency. But the blast from the explosion had rammed hard into his stomach and he was unable to use his legs.

We survivors now struggled in the water, some fifty miles from Tobruk and twelve miles from the enemy-held shore.

We had only half a Carley float between us. Into this we packed the injured until it settled so low that they were sitting up to their armpits in water. The remainder of us kept off the float, as in these conditions the injured in the float had just positive bouyancy.

Now our messdeck comedian came into his own. With great deliberation, he said, 'If Noel Coward were here I suppose he'd be singing "Roll out the Barrel" . . . Well, I bloody don't feel like singing – not even "Show me the Way to Go Home".'

It was some hours to dawn, and the uncertainty of what might or might not come with it proved too much for one man. From out of his all-night utter silence he suddenly went beserk, thus endangering the lives of the precariously situated inhabitants of the damaged raft. It needed great courage for one of the other survivors to save his fellows by hitting the crazed man with a piece of debris. The man slipped away and sank, to join those who had already died.

We soon reached the stage when some of the survivors began to lose hope of being rescued. But then out of the haze, with a great bow-wave creaming away aft, came a British motor torpedo boat.

What a sight she made coming at us. A wild cheer broke out, with mad waving of arms as she circled us, then cut her engines. Willing hands stretched down to pull us out of the water.

A search of the area was made for a while, but as we had injured men it was decided to get us back to Tobruk as fast as possible, and on the way they made us tea – there never was such tea! – and the memory of the rating in the tiny galley who stood catching the kettle as it leapt off the primus stove as we forged along is still very clear.

They cleaned us up in Tobruk, washed out our ears, gave us a bath, soaked the crude oil out of our hair – those of us who had swallowed oil were subjected to a stomach pump – and doctored the injured. My hair was so matted with oil that they cut a great deal of it off. Then, as all naval personnel in Tobruk wore khaki gear, we were issued with the same.

But there was work to do. A list of survivors had to be made out, but as so few of us had survived, from this starting-point a list of the dead could be deduced.

Then with the aid of a little rum, we slept the clock round.

Next day the same MTB took me back to the scene of the wreckage, just in case. It was truly amazing, the amount of debris spewed out of our ship – and there, among all the flotsam balancing on a six-inch plank, was a rating's wallet. It was more than likely that he had kept this in his locker, below in the messdeck; yet here it was, bobbing about in the sea, perfectly balanced on a plank.

This was all that was left of our ship and home, of the experiences, the sounds, the smells: all just memories now. As we left the scene we turned our backs sadly on an era that was so suddenly brought to a close.

Many times at our work of escorting and convoying we had witnessed the havoc and destruction wrought by a single torpedo upon a variety of ships, all considerably larger than we were. We had sought some comfort by telling ourselves that we were so small that the enemy would not bother to waste a tin fish on us. In retrospect, it seems obvious that we were torpedoed in mistake for the larger corvette, whose normal position was on the seaward quarter, which at the last moment we had been ordered to take up.

After a spell ashore our commanding officer returned to sea in command of one of the biggest frigates. Awarded a DSC he later added a bar to this when he destroyed another 'U'-boat.

The citation with my Mention In Dispatches read:

For courage and devotion to duty and disregard of his personal safety in assisting survivors to the Carley Raft. This Petty Officer's example did much to encourage and sustain the survivors during the long period they were awaiting rescue.

And *Cocker*? Her death added another hard statistic to the appalling losses of trawlers, drifters and whalers – nearly three hundred to date, by far the largest losses of any section of the fighting fleet.

HMS *Cocker* was torpedoed on 4 June 1942 by 'U'-boat 331 – the same 'U'-boat that had torpedoed the battleship HMS *Barham* some months earlier. She was thus responsible for the destruction of one of the largest ships of war and also one of the smallest.

In the end 'U' 331 was depth-charged and sunk by the Fleet Air Arm, 820 Squadron, operating from HMS *Formidable*, and the RAF 500 Squadron, North-west of Algiers on 17 November 1942.

There seemed to be a great urgency in Tobruk, lots of comings and goings. The Navy had a ship's company there and we lived with them in shelters hewn out of the solid rock. We had no duties and so took long walks out into the surrounding desert, but we were more than pleased, after three days of this sort of life, to be taken out of the harbour in a small pinnace to board HMS *Hurworth*, a 'Hunt'-class destroyer, for passage back to Alexandria.

For this passage, I was, as they say, 'Victualled' in the POs mess, and there, a member of the mess, was Freddy Broad. I had played tennis with Fred in our local public gardens just prior to the war, he married a local girl, Iris Gale, and when war finished and ex-servicemen were allocated houses he and his family came to live next door.

Small world.

We made a fast passage back to Alex where from the ship's boat we landed at No. 42 Shed: and there to meet me and tell me that Tobruk had fallen again was Billy Gilbert.

Billy was a senior naval stores officer who, although somewhat older than I was, I had known since childhood back at Portland. Knowing a SNSO had certain advantages for a coxswain, whose job it was to indent for the endless stores carried aboard ship, from paintbrushes to lavatory paper – I could, through this friendship, get things that were known to be in short supply and this did my standing among the officers a great deal of good.

Whatever the wardroom found itself short of, the cry would go up: 'Perhaps the Coxswain can help when next we get back to Alex.'

So Tobruk had fallen again, and we had only made it out of there by the skin of our teeth.

Now without a ship, and pending my next draft, I was sent to Dekelia, a rest camp on the edge of the desert, where life was so leisurely that after recent experiences it took some getting used to. Then back to Alex where I was told that, quite unknown to me, I had for the last two months been working out my probation for a commission while in *Cocker*. But my papers had been lost in the wreck so I should have to go back to sea in another ship to get new papers raised again.

In the meantime, I was sent to HMS *Saunders*, a tented camp halfway down the Suez Canal.

Time hung rather heavily here, for this was a clearing camp for survivors. All who had been rekitted out were awaiting draft; most of us were in khaki drill, which seemed foreign to us after having been in 'whites' for so long.

At this time the Army was being pushed back in the desert and, as always, some wag launched a 'buzz' that all personnel now held in HMS *Saunders* were to be made up into a Naval Division to be sent up into the desert to help plug the gap in our defences.

Whether this was a 'buzz' or not, I had no stomach for soldiering, especially soldiering in the desert, for during the few days that I had spent in Tobruk awaiting passage back to Alex I had had a close-up view of the Army at work. My admiration was unbounded, but I had decided that, in spite of having only recently been torpedoed, I would rather take my chances back at sea.

Being in a desert area, fresh water was a problem. In the camp we had the option every morning of a cup of tea or enough hot water with which to shave; We opted for the tea, drank half and shaved in what was left.

At intervals in the Great Bitter Lakes, platforms had been set up, from which small groups of men kept watch all round the clock for enemy aircraft from which mines might be dropped. On observing any splashes, cross-bearings would be taken and the position of the mine fixed.

To give me some employment, I coxswained a small power-boat whose job was to take relief crews to these platforms.

One evening, lying alongside, watching our heavily laden bombers taking off from a nearby runway, which ended abruptly where the lake began, we watched a bomber stagger into the air, lift off, but then pancake into the shallow water of the lake. The plane broke up, with debris flying everywhere, but luckily there was no explosion.

We made our way to the scene as fast as we could and, most remarkably, found the rear gunner alive in the broken-off tail-plane, but he was trapped by his legs. He was the only survivor and it took us a couple of hours to set him free.

What a lucky chap he was that the lake was non-tidal: only his head and shoulders were above the water.

Back home in Portland, it had been the nightly routine for years at bedtime for my father to go out to the front door and smoke his last pipe of the day. During this time my mother would go to bed.

Returning to the living-room, Father would rake out the fire, see everything snugged down for the night and then follow her up. By this time Mother would normally be undressed and in bed, on the night I was torpedoed, Father found her sat in the bay window fully dressed. quite convinced that 'something had happened' to me, so father said.

The Naval Division 'buzz' came to nothing and nobody was more grateful than I – and now a draft back to Alaxendria released me from the monotony of the tented camp called HMS *Saunders*.

Back at Alex I felt that I should go along to the eighth general hospital to visit the injured or survivors, a soul-destroying job, as the greater part of the patients were soldiers who had survived burning tanks, which brought back painful memories of burnt sailors we had picked up from the sea.

Our on-watch Asdic rating had survived and was not too badly injured. He described the events right up to the torpedo striking. Surprisingly, most of the on-watch personnel on the bridge had managed to get into the water, including the officer of the watch, but he must have been badly injured, for when we finally came together on the raft he was missing, but then many who may have survived the initial explosion were undoubtedly caught up in the depth-charges.

Chapter Eleven

Preliminary Selection
Board

To complete my probation for a commission all over again my
draft took me to HMS *Calamara*, as ladylike a ship as *Cocker* had
been workmanlike, as comfortable as *Cocker* had been uncomfortable, as beautiful as *Cocker* had been brutal and strong. She was,
in fact, a Greek yacht – and she was as useless as *Cocker* was useful.
It was, of course, possible that her Greek owner had offered her
to the Navy with certain provisos regarding her use and that was
possibly why we never went out of sight of land, working only
in what was called 'local patrol'.

Her accommodation, as far as naval ratings was concerned, was
sumptious! She still carried a grand piano in her wardroom and

each of the POs had a private cabin with a bathroom attached. I spent the next two months in these luxurious surroundings on probation for my commission. Next stop would be the provisional selection board.

Considering the job she did and her wartime effectiveness, *Cocker* was for me the finest experience that I could have had – the next two months were a doddle. We left harbour at 1600 most days and took up station at either 'F' or 'L' patrol for the night. By breakfast-time each morning we were back alongside. The more ribald of our friends used to say that we may as well have made fast the end of a wire to the jetty when we left every evening, steamed away, and when it became tight – that was far enough!

Certainly, after our recent duties of escort and convoy, it was rather like being drafted to the royal yacht, for we polished brass, scrubbed the decks, sandpapered lovely teak handrails, painted ship and washed paintwork over and over.

The white enamelled bathrooms in pink rose were all very pleasant but not so rewarding as being in *Cocker*; yet in some respects my work and conduct were under closer scrutiny and I was made well aware of this situation.

My CO in *Calamara* was a single-minded man, especially about his fresh cup of cocoa, served when on the bridge at sea, which he would refuse unless it had the required circle of bubbles spinning around in the middle. His steward grew tired of having to carry the rejected cup back to the galley and replace it, and in the end, just before delivering the cocoa, he would lightly spit into it to achieve the desired effect.

By now the Army had been pushed back to Alamein and all the activity in Alex suggested that, if needs be, the Navy was prepared to vacate the port – but still we did our nightly patrol and had a front-row seat for the great barrage laid down by 'Monty' when we broke out of Alamein.

I was told now to report ashore, to attend a preliminary selection board, and after much ironing and starching of a new 'white' uniform, recently purchased from a shore tailor, I presented myself at the appointed time.

Events such as this always give me butterflies in the tummy, and finding myself stood before a four-ringed captain, a commander and a couple of two-and-a-half-ringers (Lieut. commanders) was no exception. Between them they fired questions at me for a full hour – 'What is the function of an Opturating pad?', 'Explain how a Dan buoy is dropped', 'How do you think the Pyramids were built?' 'What is the purpose of a Can buoy?' what did 'at the dip' mean? or 'Orders for a boat under oars'?, 'Explain how you would take a kedge anchor away?' On and On it went. What with the importance of the interview, the heat of the day and a new well-starched uniform, by the time I got back aboard I felt as if I had been put through a mangle, and I wasn't feeling very optimistic about the outcome either.

With the rest of the crew, a windfall of seven days' leave suddenly turned up. *Calamara* had to be docked immediately, so with kitbags eagerly packed we left Alex for a rest camp at Lake Timsa (part of the Suez Canal).

How odd it was that for the whole time we were in *Cocker* we had been kept endlessly at sea, with never a stop, doing heartbreaking work – in from sea, bunker and away again – yet here in *Calamara*, doing a doddle of a job, alongside most of the time, we got seven days' leave – in a rest camp at that – there is no justice!

Lake Timsa offered us a chance of thumbing a lift down to Cairo, so after settling in to our rest camp surroundings we tried our luck, and in no time at all were picked up by a British Army truck and by a road that kept to the side of the Sweet Water Canal all the way, we did the eighty miles to Cairo, arriving extremely hot and dusty.

The problem of how the Pyramids were built was not solved by our visit; no one seems to really know how it was accomplished, although many theories exist. Having worked in quarries, I can say that the problem is truly gigantic.

Back aboard, there awaited me a signal instructing me to hand over to a newly arrived coxswain from England. I was to go to Suez not later than three days hence to take passage down to the Cape in the troopship *New Amsterdam*, to join a commissioning class at the newly opened school in Port Elizabeth.

So I had passed my PSB and was on my way to school. Having lain alongside the *New Amsterdam* when last in Durban, I remembered her to be a very modern liner and, stowing my gear when I finally joined her at Suez, I found her to be just that.

She was clean and well kept, as the Dutch had a name for keeping all their ships, with light and airy spaces. As we were making an almost empty return passage, this voyage bore no relation to my past experiences in troopships: it was all very leisurely and civilised. Back down the thousand miles of the Red Sea, round Cape Guardafui and on south, well off the African coast, through days of warm sunshine and warm breezes, at full speed and unescorted, she drove a zig-zag course to Durban.

Apart from nominal duties, there was time to spare – time to sit and read and let the mind wander back over the two-and-a-half years so far spent in the Royal Navy: the early days in HMS *Liffy*, which now seemed light years away, then the much longer time spent in HMS *Syringa*.

Both these ships had been marvellous training grounds for me. I realised that I had been fortunate to do my early training in RN ships, with professional seamen, for both these ships had been naval minesweepers, and in the early days crewed by their seamen, only later did the fishermen infiltrate into our messdeck.

Added to this 'pusser' training, I had served in a ship out of Portsmouth, our biggest naval port, where, almost unconsciously I absorbed all things naval that went on day by day. From all this I had taken on board a wealth of background that had proved valuable, all the scores of little details, access to which could only have come from the training that I had received.

How, I wondered, could I have maintained the status of coxswain in *Cocker* had not all this background and training been there to support me? And this was to apply even more so when, later on, I found myself a petty officer in one of HM destroyers (HMS *Inconstant*).

All kinds of thoughts came flooding back. On arrival at Alexandria, the pay office told me that, until my papers caught up with me, I would be paid one rank below that of PO (i.e. Leading Seaman). Somehow these papers of mine were a long time in catching up with me; consequently, I had to live in a POs mess on a leading seaman's pay for the next six months. When at last my back pay did turn up, all in one lump sum, it hardly seemed to compensate for all the months that I had spent in penury.

The story of how we 'acquired' for the *Cocker* an Italian Isotti gun that did such good service as an anti-aircraft gun came back in detail. Our engineer officer had gone ashore in Tobruk on the scrounge and from piles of artillery left by the Italians he had seen this anti-tank gun of about one inch calibre. In its original state the gun was housed on wheels. By removing these, and with a bit of skilled adapting, it was bolted down to the top of the galley and proved to be a very welcome addition to our other anti-aircraft guns.

The occasion, too, when we brought a very high-ranking, self-important Italian officer prisoner-of-war from Tobruk. He was confined to the captain's day cabin for most of the day, but was allowed to exercise under guard.

He came aboard with a mass of trunks and other baggage, all of which astonished us. The passage to Alex took longer than usual, owing to our being detached for a time to hunt a 'U'-boat. One day the Italian demanded to see our captain; protesting volubly and quoting the Geneva Convention, he complained that he had been robbed of all his orders and decorations.

He got little change out of the CO and was finally put ashore in Alex in charge of the redcaps still protesting as he flounced down the gangway.

A few days later, with the hands shaken and scrubbing down decks at five a.m. I was suddenly aware of gales of laughter. I dashed up on deck to see what was going on – and to stop it before it woke the captain. I found our tiniest A.B. and our biggest comedian, scrubbing down decks with his overalls turned up to his knees, bare-footed, but with a full dressed, plumed cocked hat sideways on his head, a marvellous blue silk sash carrying a dagger across his chest, and half-a-dozen orders and decorations pinned all over his overalls.

We had escorted decoy convoys close along the coast from Alex to Tobruk, old rustbuckets of ships that were expendable, dodging along at around six knots, to take the wrath of the enemy bombers for the whole of the 350-odd miles, while the main convoy made course as if for Malta, only altering it for Tobruk after dark, and at high speed at that.

Another of my memories is a starkly vivid picture of the messdeck in 'Syringa' the morning after what a matelot chooses to call a 'good run ashore'. The last one to lower himself down out of his hammock is 'Ginger' – there he stands in his crumpled underclothes, bleary-eyed and hair, what there is of it, all over his head, and always the same remark: 'I feel no pain, dear Mother, now, but oh, I am so dry!'

So many memories – but bowling along at twenty-five knots and all the time getting further away from the war in the Mediterranean, with only nominal duties, warm sunshine and with Durban and its very kindly people just around the corner, life seemed very pleasant.

In no time at all we were entering Durban, where, on the end of the jetty to sing us into this lovely port, was the figure known to every serviceman who passed through Durban during the war, a sort of South African Vera Lynn. All the wartime songs came floating up: 'Now Is the Hour', 'White Cliffs of Dover' and more. The 'Lady in White', as she became known, was a well-known local opera singer who was later able to claim the distinction of having sung a welcome to every troopship entering or leaving Durban throughout the war. This was the second time that I had listened to this tiny figure (for she would have been all of eighty feet below us on the dockside) and her flowing white dress and large red picture hat will be remembered by many thousands of troops from all over the world.

Durban was just as warm and friendly and welcoming, but this time we were not to stay long enough to enjoy its people's hospitality. Our destination was a large tented camp some forty five miles up in the foothills of the mountains, at Pietermaritzburg. Here, in HMS *Assegai*, we learnt that tropical routine was being worked: up at 5 a.m., school until 10.30 a.m. then, due to the heat and humidity, 'make and mend' until 2 p.m. then back to school until 6 p.m.

All this was very strange to us, but enjoyable. Everything in South Africa is big! Even their thunderstorms – and especially their hailstorms; in one storm we had to brail up the walls of the tent and, with all our gear stowed on the beds, we sat and let the water swill through the tent – hailstones which, they said were big enough to strike down cattle in the fields and kill them.

As I had spent the required time in the Middle East and had also been a survivor I was entitled to some leave. I had the choice of going to Ladysmith, Johannesburg or a farm. Being short of money – my credit at the pay office was in the region of £4 – I chose the farm. What a good choice it turned out to be.

Four of us, two ABs and two POs took a train up to a small station called Nottingham Road, where we were met by Mr Smythe, the owner of a large farm, and his son-in-law, Mr Reed. We drove out into the country and in the foothills of the Drackensburgh Mountains found their farm – called 'Delcrue' – in a lush valley. Here we spent the next fourteen glorious days, which happened to include Christmas, being entertained by this very pro-British family. They were, in fact, of Scottish descent.

The original Smythe, the father of our host, had gone out to South Africa before the Boer War and had, become the first and only Prime Minister of Natal. He died leaving each of his children, and there were several, a large farm.

It seemed that we were the first British sailors to be seen that far north, so we were shown off to all in the district. We rode horses – much to their amusement, for at best a sailor on horseback seems a bit out of place – we shot game, went to tennis parties and bathed in an ice-cool stream that filtered through their garden.

They loved to hear us talk in our several brogues, and listened eagerly to our tales of the war, from which they were so far divorced. But perhaps their greatest wonder was that we could keep ourselves so spotlessly clean in our tropical whites – and that we could darn and sew, for such menial tasks were considered out there to be beneath the dignity of white women, much less their men.

We were non-paying guests, living with half-a-dozen paying guests, all up from Durban to escape the humidity around Christmas-time. One of them, we called him Heinz, was a German, who it was said had escaped from Germany some years before war had broken out and now managed a chocolate factory in Durban. We all wondered about him! Another was a great fly-fisherman who spent all his waking hours with rod and line down by the river. His evenings were spent reading 'whodunnits' one of which had at the centre of its plot an unusual murder: the victim was hooked in the back by a fly-fisherman and played on the rod until he drowned.

We all took sides on whether this was possible and talked about it late into the night. Next morning, about a dozen of us set off down to the river to continue this ongoing argument. Being a swimmer, I was to be the 'victim'. The line was tied to my belt and I waded in. The rules of the game were that, as soon as I felt the line come tight, I could cavort around, as in fact a man would in order to free himself. It did not take long to prove that the idea was a fallacy – the line broke.

The interesting thing, however, and I was not to learn of this for many years afterwards, was that present throughout this 'try-on' was a Zulu, Mr Smythe's bearer, who had been 'given' to mine host as a boy; they had grown up together and a great deal of understanding existed between them.

What I did not know was that in general Zulus cannot swim and, what was even more strange, this particular one had never seen anyone swim and apparently stood spellbound watching me perform in the water.

Some thirty years later, our daughter, working in Africa, motored down from Botswana to these same kindly folk for a holiday. While she was with them news came that this old Zulu bearer was dying some miles away in one of the homelands'. The family decided to visit him with blankets, hot soup and other goodies, and Celia went along with them. They found him in a native rondavel.

It was explained to the old Zulu that Celia was the daughter of the man who long ago had swum in the river. He proceeded to describe the whole event, in his native tongue, which had to be translated for Celia, in great detail, which was all the more incredible as I had never told Celia this story. She heard it from this old Zulu in a tiny native hut thirty years after the event.

The fourteen days in this paradise had to end and we returned to 'Assegai' to take up our schooling once again.

A day or so before this memorable leave ended, Mrs Reed had left 'Delcrue' to go to a maternity hospital in PMB and we learnt as we left the farm that she had had a baby daughter.

For all the kindnesses that we had shared under their roof, I thought the proper thing to do would be to go along to the hospital, so, loaded with as large a bunch of flowers as I could comfortably carry, I made my way there, aware as I went along that people were staring at me.

As I entered the ward in which there were a dozen or so mothers, they all fell about laughing. It seemed – when they could find the breath to tell me – that no self-respecting South African white man would be seen carrying flowers. Yet here was what was popularly supposed to be a rum-swilling, tobacco-chewing sailor bringing flowers to someone else's wife!

I have no doubt that this story is still being told in several homes down there.

During the period back in camp, we learnt that we were to be visited by Flag Officer South Atlantic, an admiral, no less.

When the fateful day arrived, all nineteen commission and warrant candidates, as we were called – proclaimed by the wearing of a white capband – were lined up as a separate squad. Being tall, I was righthand marker. We had been schooling for some time and were, we thought, bursting with all the right answers – how to strike topmast on the *Rodney* the muzzle velocity of a fifteen inch shell, the ratio of fuel consumption from half to full speed, the weight of a bolt of canvas, and, oh, so many other answers that he was sure to seek.

All of them were flipping through my mind as the admiral approached our squad. As righthand marker, I was the first he walked up to.

He was so small that, stood to attention, I could look right over his head. He just stood and looked me up and down for what seemed like ages. The seconds went flashing by, with all the practised answers reeling around in my brain. And what did he ask me? 'Did I have any holes in my socks'? A long pause followed. I was taken completely off guard. Then – rather irritably – he asked, 'Well, don't you know? You put them on this morning.'

Thus ended my first friendly chat with an admiral.

Quite frequently our studies were interrupted by heavy storms which swept across the camp. All we could do in such situations was brail up the walls of the tents, sit with all our gear on the bed and wait for the water to sweep through and then for things to dry out. It was in one of these sessions that we took turns to recall some of the events of our stay up in Alexandria.

The Fleet Club, a haven for all naval personnel, was a totally walled-in building that offered the feeling of being cut off from the rest of the city and its noises, and at the same time reminded us of England.

The food it offered was the best and cheapest of any eating-place that a sailor could afford. Housey-housey was noisily played, with a full house winning a considerable prize, and a safe bed was always available if you ever got all-night leave.

This meant that, regardless of how well the evening had gone, Jack had to get back aboard that night and, as with all ports and docks, to get aboard Jack had to pass through the most poverty-stricken parts of the city.

A man, even a group, either walking or being transported in a 'gharry' was vulnerable to all kinds of attacks. Many servicemen will testify, drunk or sober, that muggings were commonplace out there forty or so years ago. It was for this reason that any big win at housey-housey would not be paid out at the Club, but would be delivered aboard ship next morning, as no way would a big winner be allowed to arrive aboard with that kind of cash on him.

Part of the charm of being in a foreign place is to walk its streets, smell its smells and, most of all, haggle for its bargains. This should not be hurried, and may take many days. This was especially so in Alex, with its narrow streets, the litter, the blind, the maimed the drug addicts drying-out on the pavements, the touts from the endless little shops, noisy taxis and smelly horses, orange-peel and the all-pervading smell of garlic.

It was always a great test of my stamina to have my hair cut by a barber with breath heavily laden with garlic.

The docks and harbour were enormous in Alexandria, and it

paid to remember exactly by which of the many gates you made your exit, as re-entering by the wrong gate could well give you miles to walk. Our berth was usually at No. 42 Shed, which meant that the nearest convenient gate was 22.

It mattered not by which of the many gates we left the 'gharry' drivers always took you to your destination via the infamous Sister Street. Here, throughout the war, with a city full of servicemen brisk business was carried on, so much so that queues of the kind that one might have expected to find outside an English cinema when some epic film was showing were commonplace.

As four petty officers coming off the dockside for a few hours ashore, we bargained, as was customary, with the 'gharry' driver for a price to the centre of the city, having accomplished which we finally arrived in the centre of a large square.

It was siesta time and the square was completely deserted. Further bargaining took place with the driver and while this was going on, around the back of the vehicle the horse was unshipped from the shafts, walked across the pavement, on up a flight of steps and into the foyer of a large hotel. Still not a soul about, and there in the hall stood an empty lift. The animal was backed into the lift, the doors closed and a quick exit was made.

All these years later, there still lingers a twinge of conscience but at the same time the unknown end of the story intrigues me. We wondered later, did some dear old lady on the third floor ring for the lift, when it arrived, gape in astonishment as a horse stepped out? I wish we knew.

All who have walked those streets will remember the persistence of the 'shoe-shine' boys – they were everywhere! They operated in gangs of half a dozen or so, roaming the streets in search of likely customers.

Just about the one thing a serviceman doesn't need is a shoeshine, but we were pestered just the same, until sometimes in desperation it was politic to submit, otherwise yellow slub would be thrown all over clean uniforms.

When under this kind of pressure – a form of blackmail, really – the polite expression to use to ask them to desist is 'Imshi' the Arabic word for 'Go away'. But when patience runs out the Arabic word 'yalla!' is hurled at the gang. This means 'bugger off.'

Among the particular gang who were pestering us on this day was a tall Sudanese youth. The Sudanese were more usually employed in hotels as waiters, as they were dignified in manners as well as fiercely proud of being British subjects.

Having used all the polite expressions to ask them to go away the impolite 'yalla!' was introduced at which point the Sudanese youth drew himself up to his full height and with a very pained expression said, 'You no say "yalla" to me – me British subject. You say "Bugger off!" '

A story from the 'Bunts' of HMS *Warspite*. It seems that a young AB was sent as lookout to one of the wing bridges of the battleship as she was ploughing along. In order to relieve the boredom, he was leaning against a small gun-mounting, with his shoulder under a ledge to offset the rolling of the ship, in which position he was discovered by Admiral Cunningham, coming down off his personal bridge. ABC as he was known throughout the Navy, was also known for his low-threshold temper and did not suffer fools gladly.

Placing himself in a similar position behind the rating, with shoulder under the ledge, he quietly said to him, 'You can go off watch now, I've got the weight.'

We never did get to Port Elizabeth, as expected. An emergency came up in the form of a draft to Durban, where nineteen commission candidates were to join HMS *Inconstant*, a destroyer. No prize for guessing what the Navy called her.

We were to form a steaming party to take her back to the UK. She was badly in need of the kind of repairs that could best be done in England and, as her crew had only recently arrived from home, it was decided that we should make up a party to get her back.

Her coxswain, however, was to return to England with her, so I had to be found some other job, and as my papers showed that I had a gunnery rate, I was made captain of 'A' gun, principally because no one else was either tall enough or had the power to close the breach when the gun was in depression.

The prospect was daunting, for although I had a gunnery rate I had never practised it, and now here I was captain of a gun's crew in a destroyer, more than somewhat out of my depth.

One of four destroyers, we formed up on HMS *Valliant* and set course for Cape Town, where each of the five ships loaded boxes of bullion gold for passage home. This was my first trip to the Cape. We docked at Simonstown, and had time for only one trip to Cape Town, but the railway ride alone was well worth it.

The passage up to Freetown in a destroyer, in company with a battleship, was full of new experiences for me and, being a CW candidate, I had special instruction on the bridge – all very useful.

As the 'U'-boat menace was at its worst we had little rest and, being a scratch crew, every exercise was carried out over and over again: anti-aircraft attack stations, gun drill, 'Surface-attack', 'Abandon ship', 'Submarine attack' – on and on it went, day and night.

To be part of the screen for a battleship, in a destroyer with a scratch crew so hastily assembled, was a situation no commanding officer could relish, for it normally takes many weeks of intensive shake down' training to bring any HM ship up to that standard of efficiency whereby she can, with confidence, take the full responsibility of screening a Battlewagon commanded by a Flag Officer from whom any adverse report could settle the promotion hopes of any destroyer commander.

We bunkered at Freetown, glad of the respite from ceaseless drill. Quite unexpectedly, leave to 'Watch and part' was piped. Those of us entitled hurriedly got changed into our tropical gear; this would be the last time we would be using it – in only a day now we would be needing our 'blues'.

All except chiefs and POs are inspected by the officer of the watch before being allowed ashore. This is a privilege hard won and therefore jealousy guarded.

Ashore, there seemed little to offer in Freetown, except the 'King Dick' canteen, as only a yard or so from the main street the jungle seemed to take over.

I remember buying a whole stalk of bananas and lugging it back aboard, to be much chided by the rest of the mess as, by their reckoning, we should have to bunker again before we got home, and that would have to be in the Canary Isles, in which case the bananas there were much superior.

We didn't, in fact, do so and, when we arrived in Plymouth I was the only one with bananas to take home.

A day after leaving Freetown, a large abcess appeared on my thigh and after days of pain the ship's doctor decided to lance it. I was given a general anaesthetic and woke up with rather an oversized bandage on my leg.

It seemed that, just as the doctor was poised to cut, the ship gave a bit of a lurch and I ended up with a cut much larger than was necessary – my only war wound!

Home port, Plymouth, was now only a day or so away and as it was February and we were steaming north, going on watch was decidedly chilly, and four hours of it at a time became rather painful. But soon, dead ahead, we saw the Eddystone and, just beyond that, Plymouth.

While we had been away, the Navy had trained Wrens as boats' crews and this was the first time that we had seen them in action; much ribald comment ensued.

Customs men boarded as we were coming up the Sound and each man was given a going-over in his mess. There was no escape. Seeing my bananas, my customs man asked for one for his daughter, as with wartime restrictions she had never seen one. Being able to help him I had my customs charges cancelled!

So, I had survived a Fleet destroyer and one with a typically not too amiable 'Jimmy'. Leave was piped for all Plymouth men and the nineteen commission candidates were told to catch the 9.30 a.m. train to Portsmouth.

Chapter Twelve

'Gorne Aft with the Pigs, to be an Orficer'

To Portsmouth by train. Once again we went through the interminable joining routine, made more lengthy by the fact that we had been overseas, but as soon as this was completed we were sent on leave.

Back again in Portsmouth, life was frustrating and claustrophobic after having been at sea for two years, but within a few days the nineteen of us were made up into a party and sent off to HMS *King Alfred* at Hove, in Sussex.

This was the main commissioning school for the wartime Navy and it was here that the bulk of the men commissioned from the lower deck passed out. At this time, however, so great was the need for officers to man the coming invasion fleet that a second school had been set up in Scotland.

Although every man who arrived here had already passed through several levels of testing, further rigorous tests had yet to be endured, the most important was the final selection board!

Headed by Captain Pelly, several commanders and an array of other specialist officers, it was all very daunting: to enter a room and find such an entourage of gold braid was, to say the least, unnerving. Each of us was instructed to enter the room, stand to attention and give the board our name, rank and number, followed by our length of service.

All this I smartly carried out. The entire board just sat and looked at me for what seemed an interminable age. Then the President spoke.

'Your good-conduct badge denotes that you have been in the service for three years and we note that you are a petty officer. This background suggests that you are not the material we are looking for. To have attained the rank of PO in three years is commendable – but you will, in our opinion have already formed your own standards. What we need are young men, who can be moulded to our standards, uninhibited by the lower deck!'

Well! That was deflating enough, just about equal to telling me, 'We don't like petty officers here.'

However, for the next thirty minutes, each in turn tortured me with every kind of question. I suppose being a PO for it seemed that they saw few of these here – I had opened up for them a whole new area of available questions upon which to test me. The manual of seamanship, Part Two, is a formidable tome and they could now add this to Part One in testing me.

The final test of my ability to stand my ground came when the captain, seeing that I came from Portland, asked me if I knew the Liberal Club there. I said that I lived in the same road until new premises were found in Park Road. He followed up by saying that he remembered having to go down steps to enter the club. 'With great respect, sir, you go *up* steps to get in.'

He immediately became hostile and adamant that he went down steps. I said that I had played on these steps as a boy and that they went up.

In the end he said, 'We will agree to differ!' He didn't give way: a four-ringer doesn't have to give way to a PO.

We marched and counter-marched in the streets of Hove, our

'power of command' was assessed, and mode of dress and table manners, and our officer-like qualities came under review.

Gunner's mates lambasted us with orders, for the Navy believes that you should first be able to take orders before they teach you how to give them. At any moment of the day we could be stopped, and woe betide you if any complaint could be made about your dress.

Having got this far, we were given the new psychology tests, or rather a series of them. The next morning, each of us was interviewed at some length; from the information gathered from these psychology tests I was warned of those parts of the course where I would find difficulties.

I finally passed the selection board, in spite of their not liking petty officers, but I would be going up to Lochailort, in Scotland, to do my schooling.

Lochailort, apart from requiring of us the usual scholastic attainments, was a toughening-up school, for it had been assumed that, in order to live in the conditions obtaining in landing craft, one needed a rugged personality for the spartan existence anticipated. For me, having just completed nearly two years in the Mediterranean, it was even more demanding and my introduction to Scotland in the early part of the year was a painful one.

In spite of sleeping in my overcoat, with an oilskin on top, I had never been so cold in bed in my life. We had a masochistic commander, who took great pleasure in stretching us to our physical limits, in order, it seemed, to prove that we had the 'will to win'.

All this physical effort, added to the fact that our mental capacity was also being stretched to its limits in the classroom, must have accounted for the high fall-out rate that occurred at the end of each week.

We waded through ice-cold torrents, climbed to the tops of mountains, usually in severe weather conditions, boxed, rowed the long-oared awkward naval galleys, marched in full pack, and crammed until midnight for the next day's classroom work.

Square-bashing taught us 'power to command', rifle drill made our arms ache and blistered our feet. We were cursed at, derided, demeaned by gunner's mates specially selected to knock us into shape, all this to prove our 'character'. Those of us who had already suffered a gunnery course at Chatham recognised all this for what it was, a sort of game, and let it pass over our heads.

Probably the most testing exercise, and as each followed the other they seemed to get more testing, was get to the top of a mountain called Ann Stac.

On a particularly bitter Saturday morning, with thick mist and snow, and a freezing wind, stripped down to our PT gear, it was sheer slog all the way, icy watersheds to cross, deep mud, craigs to climb – and the bitter wind had no end to it.

At the top, in a state of near-exhaustion, we had hoped for at least a pause, but who was there to meet us but our friend the commander, checking off all our names, so that no one could dodge. In weather that was now worsening, the way down was even more exhausting and dangerous – it was grim!

Many had to be helped over the final stages and not many of us were very chirpy for the next couple of days.

Then came Sunday church parade, with all the spit-and-polish. There was just no let-up.

The weeks passed, with our numbers getting thinned down at the end of each week. We climbed ropes, marched, ate our food and fell asleep. We stole coal to keep a small stove alight, around which we used to cluster to find some small relief. We wrote long essays on every conceivable subject pertaining to our course.

My favourite instructor was the schoolmaster commander, a tall, gaunt man, but with a merry twinkle in his eyes. He lectured on meteorology. Now there were many of his statements that I should have remembered, but the one that has stuck in my memory all these years was his warning as to what we might find in a rain gauge – he said, 'This is a target for men with full bladders and empty heads.'

We came to the final week, and the exam at the end of it – these weekly exams had weeded out nearly half of the original class, who had gone back to sea.

We who were left were told to pack all our gear as, whatever the results, we would all be catching the 10.30 a.m. back to London in the morning. On that final day we were told to report to the wardroom at 1530.

Here we were given the first intimation that we had passed the course, for now we were no longer addressed as 'Cadet Rating' but 'gentlemen'. Thus did we learn that we were now commissioned officers.

My mind flashed back to Lieutenant-Commander Lawson RN and I wondered if he was still in command of HMS *Cypress* and, if so, while on the one hand I had proved him wrong, on the other hand I owed him a great debt.

Away we went to our homes, a cheque for £55 in our pockets with which to buy our new uniforms, and awaited our appointments.

Mine was not long in coming. I had to report to HMS *Heldar* at Clacton as an officer under training. Having joined this shore establishment, we were further singled out as 'makee learners' by having to wear grey flannel trousers and, in place of a black necktie, a white muffler – all so that our behaviour could be monitored at all times.

Here, still convalescing from the effects of our being torpedoed, was my old commanding officer from *Cocker*. He was delighted to see me, more especially that I had completed the course that he had instigated some eleven months earlier in Alexandria.

Most of the practical work at this base was accomplished in small boats, know as LCAs (Landing Craft Assault). They had done fine work in the Middle East, especially at Tobruk, so they were no strangers to me.

They were twin-screwed and could be run silent, for stealing into enemy beaches. The could also be operated with just one stoker and a coxswain and for the purposes of our training the Officer was the coxswain. Daily we took these boats out into the estuary in groups of six and did all the usual manoeuvres using 'red and blue' forms (red for port, blue for starboard – green flags, the normal for starboard, are hard to distinguish at any distance). It was all great experience and not without its fun, for once out of sight of the base, we would beach in all sorts of odd places, especially those with a pub nearby.

The remainder of the training was watchkeeping and as I had done a great deal of this in *Cocker*, it was a doddle. Under the watchful eye of a very severe 'Jimmy', some semblance of what he called 'officer-like qualities' was gained, for although we had attained the status of an officer our manner of dress reminded us, and everyone else, that we were still under training and accordingly the most onerous jobs were awarded us.

Only after six weeks of this did the Navy allow us out of this sort of 'purdah' to dress normally.

From the kind of training and the sort of boats in which we worked, it soon became obvious that our purpose in any future invasion would be to land infantry and be at the very thrust, perhaps even ahead, of the invasion to carry out sneak raids on the enemy coast.

The story was told of how an officer with one stoker had recently entered Boulogne and wearing some sort of disguise, walked up on the pier, where a German band was playing. Somehow they got a German officer to return with them to the boat, where they slugged him and brought him back as a prisoner!

While still working at Portland, before I joined up, part of the very interesting work I did was loading stone from Castletown pier. This was arduous work, controlled by the tides and making no allowance for the weather – once a ship had been started it had to be finished, daylight or dark. Among the many ships loaded between 1930 and the time I joined up was a large steel barge owned by Everard and called *Britannic*.

She stands out in my memory not only because of her size but because she had a most piratical skipper – fierce black eyes, a drooping moustache and gold earrings. He fascinated me.

On this occasion, we had gone out into the estuary, where we spent some time doing our usual evolutions before being caught in a heavy rainstorm. The only available shelter was a Thames barge lying at anchor nearby. Waving us aboard was a lone figure. How glad we were to pack ourselves down into the tiny cabin, where we found, of all people, the piratical skipper, earrings and all. We drank strong tea and talked of Portland and the big Everard barges.

Later, we were made up into flotillas, at which time our crews joined us and we became known as 'boat officers'. Soon – now minus our boats – we moved down to Plymouth to join HMS *Foliot* out at Roborough Down.

Chapter Thirteen

The Gilbert and Sullivan Era

Further training was now devised. In the first place we had to lick our crews into physical shape, which was done with the aid of a particularly vicious assault course, long country runs and forced marches.

The assault course was designed to move along a valley and criss-cross a turbulent river. We did this course every day. We swung from trees, slithered down wet ropes, crossed over on a single plank, vaulted and learnt to monkey across on a single rope; the penalty for one foot wrongly placed was total immersion in very cold water – not very funny, as it was now November. All this and we never saw a boat.

In camp we lived a very spartan life, just one bucket of coal per week: other fuel had to be scrounged from the woods. The coal dump was wired-off, but some of the more enterprising ratings 'found' their way in after dark and happily filled extra buckets for their mates and passed them over the top.

But not for long. A careful trap was laid by the authorities and a lone rating was caught redhanded. His name was Barlow. We had all made up our minds about Barlow long ago, hoping that he would not be drafted to our particular ship. In due course he came up before the 'Bloke', a fatherly old sea-dog who claimed to have been to sea, as a boy, in HM ships that still carried sail. He took great delight in reciting the old order, 'Down funnel, up screw, make all plain sail'. He had probably been chopped by the 'Geddes' axe way back in 1926 (so called after the Minister held mainly responsible for that year's swingeing cuts in Navy strength), when he was a warrant gunner; he now sported two-and-a-half rings.

Out from under his battered cap stuck tufts of silver hair and a large, florid but kindly face, weather-beaten in the extreme, as if he had spent his enforced retirement from the Navy on the seafront. The rest of his uniform seemed to be kept up by the fact that his trousers were always tucked into his welly boots.

Within all this, however, was a man who understood men and dealt with them not so much on strict Naval lines but rather in a more Gilbert and Sullivan manner, making the punishment fit the crime.

We all wondered just what punishment he would dish out to Barlow, who Navy-style would have been awarded extra work in the 'dogs', or perhaps loss of pay. But this wise old owl came up with a Solomon-type solution: Barlow had to double away to his mess and get changed into his best No. 1 suit and report back to the officer of the day.

Then he was taken back to the coal dump, with instructions that he was to keep watch on the dump until he caught the next thief, only then, when he had brought the new culprit to the officer of the day would he be relieved. News of this novel treatment quickly spread around the camp and the loss of coal was soon reduced to a minimum.

Another of his ploys: a seaman named Price was caught for a very minor offence, cap flat-a-back, or smoking out of 'stand easy'. He was brought before the 'Bloke' in a highly nervous state, for he was not of the jack-my-hearty sort and has visibly suffered all night at the thought of being punished. As he stood before the punishment table, both the 'Bloke' and the master-at-arms were aware of this situation. The master read out the charge.

'What have you got to say?' asked the 'Bloke'.

'Nothing,' whispered Price.

Then, in a stage whisper to the master, the 'Bloke' said 'What did we do with the last one?' With a twinkle in his eyes, the master replied, 'We had him shot, sir.'

'Then shoot this one,' ordered the 'Bloke'.

The commanding officer of the good ship *Foliot* was a four-ringer (captain) and obviously a sea-going type. Rumour had it that he had been beached for some irregularity and he made it clear in no uncertain manner that this appointment had not been at all to his liking.

He wore a monocle, and rode a pony three sizes too small for his quite large frame. As officers of the watch, we all dreaded the first watch – it was usually during the latter part of this watch that he returned from the local hostelry and nightly would lead the poor OOW a dog's life.

One of his drunken tricks was to sway along to his cabin, which the OOW had already blacked out, fling back all the blackout curtains, switch on all the lights, then yell for the OOW, who would be publicly berated for his inefficiency.

We had very little choice but to put up with this sort of thing. But enough was enough. He must have thought he was having an attack of the DTs when drunk again, he reached his cabin, no doubt to play his mad game once again, only to find it occupied by his horse . . . Things went quiet for a while – perhaps we were taking a leaf out of the 'Bloke's' book and making the punishment fit the crime.

After weeks of physical training we had several hundred officers and men all bubbling over with exuberant health. The problem was how to contain all this pent-up energy. We ran across country every day, did assault courses, played football, force-marched by the mile – and all this so that one day we could storm up some enemy beach which seemed more like a job for the Army!

The weeks went by and suddenly it was Christmas; it was to be the first Christmas that I would be spending ashore since the war had begun.

Now, the custom in the Navy on Christmas Day is for all officers to dress as sailors and to wait at table on the ratings. We went one step further – we dressed a likely rating in officer's kit, introduced him to the wardroom as having joined that day – and everyone stood him a drink in sympathy for having had to travel on this festive day.

This went on until we began to doubt if the rating could stay the course, but he did, and we put him to bed snoring and not knowing if it was Christmas or Easter.

That night, supported by a couple of others, I climbed the fifty-foot flag-mast on the quarterdeck and impaled a chair on the lightning conductor at the very top.

Next morning at Divisions, it was hilarious to watch the effect upon the staff as they stood stiffly to attention, their eyes ascending with the ensign to the peak, and there at the truckhead was a chair.

As it was Christmas we got away with it and not too many questions were asked, although all who took part could have been named.

It was now becoming obvious that some sort of crisis was looming up, for all the boats that we were supposed to man were nowhere in sight – and we were running out of enthusiasm. But suddenly all boat officers were on draft to Troon, in Scotland, where we were to begin a course for first lieutenant in major landing craft.

I distinctly remember a feeling of great relief in getting out of minor landing craft, which were to be taken over by the Royal Marines.

Just a few weeks before getting this draft the padre at *Foliot* had been drafted there, so at least we should have a friendly face to welcome us. Little did we know that, quite unwittingly, the padre had, whilst he was having his breakfast, said, on reading the attachment list: 'My, but this is a bunch of skates we have arriving tomorrow.'

The 'Jimmy', hearing this off-the-cuff joke, took it quite seriously and as we stepped off the train he met us personally, and in no uncertain terms made it clear that he would not tolerate any sloppiness, whether in dress or conduct, and warned us that from now on our caps had to contain a 'grommet', top button done up at all times, and, however we had behaved in our last ship, forget it! He ran a tight ship and its name was HMS *Dinosaur*.

We wondered what had hit us, and smarted under this undeserved attack. Our new shore-base was a very large hotel now commandeered by the Navy. It faced straight out into the Firth of Clyde. Away to port was Alsia Craig, with the Isle of Arran straight ahead. They say in that part of the country that 'If you can see Alsia Craig, it's going to rain; if you can't it's raining.' How right we found that to be.

Right in front of the hotel we had our own golf links. In fact, there were several in the area. But we had no time to play golf, though we did use the links to endlessly practice our 'red and blue' turns, invariably accompanied by a flock of sheep.

Picture the scene: a chief yeoman of signals, in charge of twenty or so officers, out on the golf course, in four columns of five: we represented a squadron of ships at sea.

The yeoman, by using a system of signals, can wheel or turn us as a body. He has lived signals all his life, while we have to transpose his orders as we go along and obey them at the executive order 'Down'.

To what seems like a simple system at the outset, all kinds of variations can be applied, and in no time at all we are about as organised as the flock of sheep that insisted on following us around.

This alone could provoke the yeoman to all kinds of witticisms. He had been bred to think and talk nothing but signals, so he couldn't begin to understand why we lesser mortals were unable to carry out his simple instructions.

The days were fully occupied with classroom studies. The weather was as reasonable as Scotland can produce at that time of year and our recently acquired physical fitness was allowed to lapse.

Here for the first time we came into contact with the monsters to which we had been appointed as 'Jimmys'. We spent days at sea trying to master their idiosyncrasies, of which there were many. To make an error of judgement with the 'ahead' speed meant disaster, for even with main engines at full astern, they continued to slide forward: they had so little draught that they had no grip on the water.

We carried out every evolution in the book, including our much-practised 'red and blue' turns. We slammed our way back to Brodick Bay, in the Isle of Arran, coming home wet, weary and hungry day after day; then, for a rest day, we competed again on the golf course, with the sheep and our 'red and blue' turns.

On a rather fine Sunday afternoon the padre, thinking that he had been responsible for our unfortunate introduction to *Dinosaur*, decided to make amends by inviting six or seven of us to walk with him right down the length of the golf links and on to Prestwick, where he would buy us tea in a very fine Dutch tea house.

We should have taken his offer as it was meant, but we thought that this time was just the opportunity to get out own back on him. So instead of ordering just tea and cakes, as had been intended, we ordered plaice and chips as well, and ran him up a bill that at the time was quite embarrassing to him.

We all thought this was hilarious and ribbed him all the way back to base; in fact we cherished the joke for days, thinking we had put one over on him.

Upon receipt of our first mess bill, however, each of us found to our great humility, that mess chits for whisky, to the precise value of the tea, had been signed for by the padre and added to our bills. So he had the last laugh after all.

The problem of handling the LCTs became more acute when the time came to enter harbour, especially when that harbour was Troon and the ship in question was a Mark 3 LCT. They were the most unwieldly of craft and made more so when entering the small gap at Troon with adverse winds and tide.

Troon had all these complications and a few more of her own making, for as soon as the craft had passed through the gap to its pivot point, in order to avoid running straight into the shipyard opposite, the wheel had to put hardover to port – 'full astern port', 'slow ahead starboard'.

This had the effect of almost making her stand up on her rudder post and at the same time claw round to port.

With a lot of praying, she would come round, but it needed nerves of steel and quite a bit of bravado to even attempt this manoeuvre, especially as there were times when identical ships, under the same conditions, would react in completely different ways. It was only by continually handling a ship in every permutation that her behaviour could be anticipated.

Taking a ship into Troon was part of every aspiring officer's training, and a very nerve-racking one it was, for any misjudgement, especially of speed, and a great deal of damage would be done to the shipyard. Being thrown in at the deep end seemed to be part of the test of our endurance, but it must have broken the nerves of more than a few trainees.

My appointment was to stand-by for one of the new Mark 4s now being built at Middlesbrough.

Chapter Fourteen

Shake Down

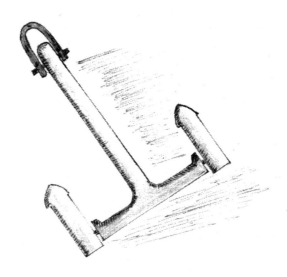

To stand by an uncompleted ship was an experience to be remembered – not enjoyed, or looked forward to, but endured.

The debris in the builder's yard was everywhere: great heaps of anchor chain, piles of coils of wire rope, ship's boats, bollards, stacks of steel plates, great puddles of water, rusty gangways, bales of waste – all this and more seemed to fill every available space. Then there were heavy fenders, grass ropes, signal gear, chain strops, buckets, brooms, messtraps, soap, toilet paper and all the endless articles that go to service a ship.

The multitude of stores, all of which had to be signed for, had as yet no lockable stowage space. There were no lights, no running water, no heat for cooking, no toilets. The crew, who we had yet to get to know, were living in a far-away hostel, which gave them every excuse to be late arriving each morning. Then they had to change into their overalls, and by the time that was done someone would want to go to the toilets, and these were right over on the other side of the dock. Then it was time for 'stand easy'; and when they did start work they were not at all happy about lugging great coils of wire rope from the stores, which were also far away across the docks.

All this happened in some of the worst weather which that so-called spring could find that year. Wet boots, no hot food, up and down gangways, then trudging miles back to the hostel, did not make for a very happy crew with which to begin our shakedown.

At this point the ship was not much more than a hulk, nothing yet with which any sort of pride could be associated; the work was drudgery, hard and manual, and the more we tried to keep the endless shipyard debris down the more seemed to arrive.

Planks, welding sets, with a maze of electrical leads, red lead paint, shipyard 'maties' and anchor-chains, filled every space. As yet we had no galley facilities. Our main engines were being lowered into the bowels of the ship through great gaping holes in the deck. Gunner's mates were bolting down gun rings, signal ratings were fixing flag lockers, wheelhouse telegraphs were being tested. Voice-pipes, handrails and anchors all seemed to be arriving at the same time.

Each item had to be signed for in a dirty dockside hut, and all this was to continue until our shipboard accommodation was habitable. But day by day some progress was made and the ship grew slowly into something more like a ship and less like a hulk.

At last the day arrived when we could move aboard and finally get some control over matters, especially in shaking the crew into something like ship's routine and discipline.

Now we could see the day, not far away, when we would be going on our trials, first the basin trial and, if this was successful, sea trials. A daily routine could be worked out and adhered to, so that on the day laid down we could achieve the aim that we had all been working for, that of taking her to sea.

Finally, with a complete coating of Admiralty-grey paint on, we broke out a brand-new white ensign, topped-up with fuel and ammunition and were 'In all respects ready for sea'.

We said goodbye to Middlesbrough and sailed south. The weather was kinder now, the sun came out and there on the high cliffs away to starboard was Scarborough, with all its memories, among them of having gone into the beach in a ship's boat from

Syringa to tow off a mine. All that was three years ago now. Later, up came Whitby Abbey and then Flamborough Head, with its memory of the old fisherman and his gift of lobsters, of 'E-boat alley' and the bomb-happy days spent on the lower deck.

No time was lost in shaking down both ship and crew into a fighting unit. To do this we endlessly carried out every evolution in the manual, both day and night, for we knew that by the time we joined up with our squadron, wherever that might be, we would be expected to be a well-oiled machine, with the ship's company fully shaken down. For we could expect endless beachings as soon as we joined our sister ships.

All the 'bugs' that are to be found in the complex organisation of running a working ship – beaching, unbeaching, raising and lowering the heavy tank door – had to be worked at until each evolution, daylight or dark, ran like silk. These were the specialised duties of landing craft. All the usual duties of keeping the ship at sea under wartime conditions, and fighting as required, had to come as second nature.

The greatest hazard was keeping the ship at sea in all weathers without the help of lighthouses and lightships, which are so necessary in peacetime – no small undertaking for the hundreds of 'amateurs' like myself who, with only three years' experience at sea, had, with the heavy responsibility imposed upon us so early, learnt quickly to 'smell' our way along in dark or foul-weather conditions.

We had now to prepare ourselves to be able to load and discharge a full complement of tanks in all weathers, thick o' fog or flat o' calm, and none of us knew just how long we would have to do so.

By now we were abreast of Great Yarmouth and our engines were showing signs of overheating, so we entered and spent a day rectifying this problem.

Our next stop was Southend pier, where we received instructions to join up with a convoy for onward passage through the straits of Dover. This was to be a night passage in very restricted channels, with no shore navigational lights to guide us, a green ship's company and in convoy formation.

Some of our seamen could not yet be trusted to take a turn at the wheel – and yet we would be expected to keep close station through probably the most restricted channel in the world. Our coxswain and one other could steer a good course, so these two were reserved to take the wheel after dark, or as long as it took to get past the narrows.

The gods smiled on us that night – we made a quiet passage, one not without its problems but at least when daylight came up we were somewhere near our original station in the convoy and not completely blind from watching the dim blue light at the stern of the ship ahead.

How pleased we were to see the dawn, and breakfast tasted particularly good that morning, for it seemed that the Admiralty had made a wager with us that, for the princely sum of £19 per month, we could not take this new ship, full of 'bugs' from Southend through the straits of Dover, with the greenest of ship's companies, after dark, in convoy formation and devoid of any help from any shore or navigational aid; and we had won.

By now we had spent several full days and nights at sea. Possibly the powers-that-be knew full well that the best and only place for a sailor to learn his trade is at sea, so they kept us going. Off Portland we received a signal informing us that our destination was Milford Haven; weather permitting, we would be at sea for a few more days and nights yet.

Rounding Land's End, we began our final leg in fine style, but soon the sky to the south-west took on a greasy look and at sunset ominous 'sun dogs' were visible – these usually foretold wind.

To confirm this the glass began to drop, so we ran on with the distinct possibility of a SW gale overtaking us.

Our northerly course would give us a corkscrew motion, so we battened down, and by the middle watch the wind had begun to pipe. By dawn the sky was leaden and rain swept in great squalls.

'When rain comes before wind, halliards, sheets and braces mind' went the old sailor's ditty and wise we were to tour the ship and give every bottle-screw a further turn, check every lashing and tighten every cover.

Breakfast in the messdeck was chaotic, as by now she was sliding about like a drunken pig. This was going to be no short blow, so with a prayer we ran for the lee of Lundy Island.

It was noon before we found the comfort of this lee and in the process learnt more than enough of the characteristics of our flat-bottomed craft.

One thing was certain – running before a SW gale there was no way we could maintain our northerly course. Her head blew off and a ten-degree weather helm did nothing to help the problem, which was lack of grip in the water, for in our unloaded state we only drew twenty-seven inches of water, while the wind's effect on our five feet of freeboard was to crab us along sideways. We counted ourselves lucky that there had been a Lundy Island to hide behind, for to have punched into this gale would surely have broken our back. How grateful we were to drop anchor in quiet waters. Some thirty-six hours were to pass before the gale blew itself out and we could proceed to Milford Haven.

We went up-river at Milford to Nayland and from here, in the days that followed, we tried out every function of the craft. The heavy exit door was our main tribulation. It could be well controlled in the lowering, but to hoist it back and secure it for sea was another matter. All this was back-breaking work which had to be done by the hand-winches under the forecastle.

Tanks and all kinds of other vehicles were loaded from all kinds of beaches, transported several miles along the coast and then discharged on some other beach. Our full load was twelve of the largest type of tank. We watched in amazement as the drivers of these great animals backed them along the tank deck into the two-abreast position in the tank hold. Once in position, each tank had to be union-screwed down to prevent any movement should we meet bad weather. This too was heavy work for the crew.

The build-up to D-Day was hotting up – no leave or 'make and mends', the ships and crews were kept at it endlessly, day and night.

Our living conditions were at best spartan. A metal box, about twelve feet by eight feet served as a wardroom, to be shared by two officers.

At night our blankets were unstowed from the wardrobe and a bed made up on the daytime seats. The table, if one wished to use the wardrobe, had to be unshipped – while the handbasin was the brainchild of no less than a genius. After use it was tilted upwards and backwards so that the dirty water was emptied into a galvanised container. An eye had to be kept on the level of the water in the container, otherwise it would end up all over your feet. All it needed was a length of pipe and a bit of plumbing and the whole problem could have been shot over the side. But these craft were built down to a price and not up to a standard.

The crew's accommodation was literally among the Paxman Ricardo engines, enormous diesels, quite deafening when we were under weigh. How men lived in such conditions, conducted conversations or wrote letters, was a mystery.

We all felt that the impending move back to Plymouth was part of the D-Day assembly plan and when we arrived in the river Tamar we were not surprised to find the place brimming over with every conceivable kind of craft, so much so that there was little room in which to move around.

Having found a trot buoy to moor to, it was even more difficult to move away from it to go and store ship, as we had to do. Each in turn was called into a basin to get the new 'Mulock Extensions' welded on to the already weighty tank door, apparently a last-minute brainwave which allowed us to discharge our cargoes on a more shelving beach than was possible before.

The idea looked alarming but it worked, it would be interesting to know just how many crushed fingers and black nails resulted from having to manhandle these contraptions, up and over, whenever we raised or lowered the door – they were an abomination to the crew and after only a few beachings they became so distorted as to be useless, so, with the help of a sledge-hammer, we knocked them off and dumped them into the sea.

Other than this we had little to do except clean and paint ship. After so much unending activity in the recent past, this was welcome.

We painted a large 'Q57' on the face of the bridge. This was our squadron number and it began to look as if we should be loading for the big event shortly.

Quite suddenly, however, we were singled out and, with one other LCT sailed to Portland on detached service, where we found that we had been seconded to the Americans and would be taking their assault engineers in on D-Day.

But before we arrived at what was my home port, with all the documentation involved in Operation Overlord relevant to us safely aboard, we were forced into Dartmouth with a duff port engine. This matter proved so serious that it was decided to replace the entire engine, which meant that all the port-side deck plates above the engine had to be removed and the engine lifted out.

Under a large crane a new engine was fitted – with all speed, for the undertaking was not without its panic and by the time we had done basin trials a week had gone by. We left Dartmouth and, unescorted, made all haste across Lyme Bay to Portland. What easy pray we would have been for any E-boat, and what a prize we would have been, with all our D-Day operation documents aboard!

Immediately on arrival we went alongside and loaded General

Grant tanks, each of which weighed eighty tons, and with their crews we now had a full house. It certainly wasn't boring waiting for Eisenhower to say, 'Let's go' for we sat in the wardroom listening to our Yankee passengers telling their fascinating stories. We were, of course, confined to ship now that the operation documents had been read. Our great worry was that we now had some sixty people aboard to feed and water. If we didn't go soon, we would have a problem.

As all the world now knows, we did go and although the water problems, in particular, became acute, the food situation was never difficult, for our American friends were so generous with their 'K' rations, the like of which we had never seen before.

They were in sealed cardboard boxes, waxed and numbered one to ten, so that each day a different numbered box could be chosen, providing a complete change of diet. Self-heating soups – just the thing for night watches – a whole variety of tinned cheeses, bars of chocolate, jams, biscuits and all kinds of tinned meats – even a packet of lavatory paper – were included in each box. No check seemed to be made on how many were opened, or who by, and when the tank crews finally left us on the beaches in Normandy, we were left with dozens of unopened boxes of these rations; as each contained rations for ten men for one day we were to be stocked up with food for weeks to come.

As things turned out, we had need of all these leavings, for, having discharged our first cargo, we were commandeered by the beach authorities and for the next few days provided a ship-to-shore shuttle service.

However, that is getting ahead of the story.

Chapter Fifteen

Tramlines to Omaha Beach

We chugged out of Portland Harbour in droves and, being detached from our squadron, enjoyed the freedom of making our own way up to St Catherine's-Point in the Isle of Wight and then to 'J' area, where we altered course for the beaches.

Park Lane at the rush-hour had nothing on this area of the sea that day. With a freshening wind, a lumpy sea developed and by now our American tank crews had gone very quiet and not a little green around the gills.

We were now surrounded by great masses of ships coming out of Southampton and Portsmouth hundreds of all kinds of craft, among them great slab-sided monsters built of solid concrete, wallowing along behind fussy tugs: what on earth could they be for?

Never had such an armada set out. It became known as 'the Longest Day'. We punched on, now wet, and even if it was June it was cold, with angry seas splashing over the tank deck, much to the annoyance of our Yankee passengers.

Our course was now south Four east, and it was not until Cap Barfleur came abeam that we began to feel the lee of the land, and pushed on into calmer waters.

There must have been many soldiers who at this stage would have agreed with the official publication when it referred to 'the Tank Landing Craft, as they are called, square-nosed, unwieldy, on board which living conditions must reach almost the highest degree of discomfort afloat.'

The sea was full of ships, all moving inexorably towards dawn and the beaches. At dawn we saw that the 'battle wagons' were wearing their battle ensigns, so we broke ours out, too: after all, we would be getting in close enough to see the whites of their eyes, while the 'big fellers' would be lobbing their fifteen inch bricks over our heads as we went in to discharge our tanks on the beach.

With dawn breaking, it was a great comfort to have them providing us with their umbrella.

The masses of landing craft now veered off to starboard, and then, as if in a review at Spithead, split into the appropriate squadrons for their allotted beaches.

'Omaha' and 'Utah' were the codenames given to the American beaches, the first ones reached. The British beaches were 'Sword', 'Juno' and 'Gold' but, having been seconded to the Americans, we used only the American beaches throughout the entire campaign.

This day has been written of in so many other places. The great traditions that backed us up, the training, the thinking, the planning, and the execution – they were all coming to fruition here this morning.

The immensity of the event became evident as the day wore on, when entire harbours began to take shape – those leviathan floating concrete blocks that none of us had been able to guess the reason for. We had brought our own harbours with us.

The impossible had become a fact before our very eyes and men and equipment were being piled ashore both day and night.

Way down between the American and British sectors there were high cliffs and the majestic old *Warspite* was hurling eight-gun salvoes at the enemy gun emplacements sited at the top of them. That was something to remember!

Finally our water supply ran out and we were released from this endless ship-to-shore shuttle; we had been hauling that blasted tank-door up several times a day for the past seven days.

How glad we were to see Portland again and to tell our contemporaries of the night that we were ordered alongside HMS *Rodney*, to act as a plug ship for the night, and how at dawn she had fired a full salvo with us alongside.

The various 'hards' at Portland were alive with movement and great activity: tanks, and every other kind of vehicle, with all their requirements, were being loaded into the waiting LCTs. As each loaded vessel drew away, its place was taken by another, sliding into the ramps, tank-doors lowered ready to receive all the paraphernalia of war.

Each tank, as it was positioned aboard, had to be scotched and secured with chain strops, and then union-screwed down for the voyage to the beaches; this latter was the duty of the crew, as was water ship, store ship, refuel and replace any faulty item, all this in the short time that was spent on the 'hards' loading.

It was backbreaking work for the crew, and all the physical training that we had endured now began to make sense. Then we drew off to a buoy and awaited the time-honoured signal that was always prefixed with the words, 'Being in all respects ready for sea,' etc.

This was how the build-up was accomplished. The harbour seemed to be full of these ungainly craft – workmanlike, plodding backwards and forwards to the beaches day and night.

Based at Portland, we had around 300 miles to steam for a round trip and, of the three main departure-points, we had by far the most exposed passage to make. For these waters of the Channel during spring tides are notorious for the effect of being squeezed between the Cherbourg Peninsular and Portland Bill. Add to this total exposure to the pounding of a south-westerly gale and some idea may be gained of the permutations of problems that had to be faced.

The area is renowned for its summer gales, but we were fortified by the knowledge that these crafts were not designed to be sailed in more than force four winds – so we were told, though this was totally ignored once the invasion had begun.

We battled back and forth, day and night, from June until the end of November and in all chalked up twenty-three round trips.

We enjoyed being on detached service, for there were many advantages in this state of affairs, not the least being the endless supply of 'K' rations.

Often we sailed back from the beaches on our own, as opposed to being in convoy, and we would cut corners and, when spring tides were favourable, romp back direct from Barfleur to Portland instead of keeping to the correct channel, north of the Isle of Wight, then west to Portland.

No one seemed to mind, as the task in hand was to do as many trips as possible and now that the Army had gained a foothold it was important that they be kept well supplied.

It all began by someone suggesting that we run an unofficial 'Blue Riband' among the hordes of LCTs for the greatest number of round trips to the beaches and back. It would add a bit of edge to what had become the boring to-ing and fro-ing. The authorities turned a blind eye, as it was felt that a bit of healthy competition could only help to make the build-up more effective.

But, as always, the really wide boys will take any risk in cutting the corners. After disembarking our load, instead of going to the appointed area to join up with a homeward convoy via the swept channel, we waited until dark, then hared up under the coast to Cap Barfleur and set a course for Portland. Crossing the odd minefield didn't trouble us, as we only drew twenty-seven inches unloaded. The establishment, seeing that the Army was well on its way to Berlin, decided to tighten things up, as they had got a little out of hand. But finding ourselves at the top of the unofficial 'league'; we were driven to distraction to maintain our position when stealing up to Barfleur and then full speed for home became complicated by instructions that a 'sanctuary area' north of Cherbourg had to be kept free of all shipping until 0300 hours, to permit our MTBs to have an uncluttered field in which to take on any lurking E-boats. Obviously a necessary precaution for the safety of the slow LCT convoys – but, equally, it would hamper our 'contest'.

On one occasion, with the help of spring tides we thought we could run the gauntlet. The complete calm and velvety darkness would help us and, feeling like a small boy about to steal apples, we left Barfleur and, with our skirts held high, ran with a spring tide full speed for home.

Then it happened – a starshell burst right above us, and way out to port an Aldis lamp demanded: 'What ship.'

It was as if we had been caught with our bag of stolen apples.

We knew that this spelt TROUBLE but, not unnaturally, the shock seemed to quicken our brains. Remembering that our buddy ship was on the slips at Poole under repair, we sent her number . . . It seemed to satisfy them and we continued our passage to Portland, but for some days afterwards every signal brought a sort of tingling to the hair at the back of the neck.

Days passed and we seemed to be getting away with our deception. It was some ten days later, when our buddy ship joined us from Poole, that we learnt how complete our deception had been. While on the slips at Poole they had been boarded by a provost-marshal in the person of a Royal Marines major, who demanded to know what they were doing within the 'sanctuary area' before 0300 on a certain morning. An inspection of their log got them off the hook and we laughed ourselves to sleep for a week.

Chapter Sixteen

Lee Shore

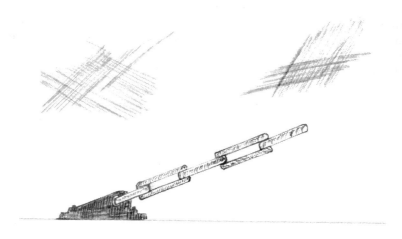

How wise it was to have let the build-up run on through our efforts in the 'Blue Riband' league, for on 'D plus 19' a quite unprecedented south-easterly gale of enormous ferocity for the time of year nearly wrecked the whole show. It was the kind of setback that no planner could have dreamed of and its effect was devastating.

Sunset had been greasy, with a calm ominous to all seagoing men. Anchoring in close company with the hordes of craft off Omaha beach did little to help our peace of mind.

The glass was dropping, but what harm could there be in that? A blow from the so'west gave us a weather shore, with the land protecting us.

Besides, it was June and we comforted ourselves with the

thought, better be anchored off these beaches in a so'west gale than be lying in many of the South Coast harbours.

We turned in, making sure that the stern anchor was leading free. As the night wore on, the air in the tiny wardroom grew thick, and sleep was hard to come by. Condensation ran down the bulkheads and dripped off the deckhead and the irritating 'pop-pop' of the generator and its accompanying vibrations only added to the tension.

The never-failing 'tell-tale' of worsening weather, when at anchor in an LCT was the thumping up and down on the quarter-deck of the heavy bulldog grip that held the anchor wire; the rhythmic crashing on the steel plates could hardly fail to wake the heaviest sleeper.

The warning could not be ignored, but what we did not know was that it heralded what was to be a south-east gale of unprecedented ferocity for high summer. It nearly ruined all the invasion efforts to date.

We were up long before dawn and did not need to be told that, from the very feel of the wind, this was going to be something quite special. From the direction of the south-east we no longer had the comfort of a weather shore, but the far more ominous 'lee shore' was staring us in the face.

Dawn only confirmed all these fears and, with the glass falling, conditions could only deteriorate as the day progressed.

Already those craft anchored close to the shore were beginning to feel the effects of the swell that was building up and rolling in from seawards onto this shallow shore and increasing in both size and weight.

There was a thrumming in the rigging, with the ensign cracking and tugging at the halliards. A peculiarity of LCTs was to anchor by the stern, to accommodate hauling off the shore upon which we had deposited our cargo; but it also presented a large, flat transome to the running seas which produced a jolting and a snatching on the anchor wire.

We knew, from experience, that this could not be allowed to continue without the possibility of the wire cable parting; if this should happen, someone could be seriously injured.

The whole atmosphere was now charged with vicious power and those of us who had lived by the sea knew by the feel of it that we were in for a real blow – but from the SE? In June? Almost unheard-of.

At noon it was still dark and, with engines going half-astern to ease the strain on the anchor cable, we waited for enough room to up anchor and get the hell out of it. The risk was frightening – too frightening for many – but with the lee of a Liberty ship to help us, at emergency 'full astern' we bucked into a rising sea.

Still using the lee of the Liberty ship, we brought her broadside into the wind as we broke out the anchor.

Now, with 'full ahead together' and hard to port, would she come up into the wind? Being deeply laden helped and we drove out of the lee, up into the gale! Did our engines have the power to sustain her way through the water? The staggering weight of wind fought us every inch of the way, but slowly, slowly we won round and at snail's pace punched through the gale out into deep water.

By now we had a big south-easter, with poor visibility and low, scudding clouds making it more like dusk than noon, but with the comforting thought that we had escaped the immediate trap, and with time to survey the beaches in detail, we were surprised at the chaos that had so rapidly built up – it was quite unbelievable.

Comparatively speaking, we now seemed to have the sea to ourselves; with plenty of fuel, we adopted the ploy of punching into the wind for a couple of hours, making only painful headway, then dropping the anchor and letting her drift slowly back. This way we had at least an hour or so of a spell. We repeated this over and over again.

Conditions on deck made it wet and dirty work. The craft was sluggish and the crew with no experience of this kind of gale, were showing signs of strain under the everlasting stress. Add to this the spartan conditions in which they were forced to live, the unseemliness of all the broken ships, the noise of the gale and all the flotsam of war, the cold, the wet and the lack of sleep, and it all began to feel as if the grounded ships might have a certain advantage over us.

Then, some time during the night, while dropping back on our dragging anchor, it must have fouled – and the wire parted.

Luckily, no one was hurt. We were right back in trouble again. The storm tore at everything in its path and being on deck in such conditions became a physical torment.

The task of shackling up the only other anchor (a light bower anchor), which was kept lashed on the forecastle, was delayed until daylight, so we dodged the gale for the rest of the night. It was a labour-intensive job to take the end of the spare anchor-wire through the after bullring, then right forrard, outside everything, and get it shackled onto this light anchor; having shackled it on, we knew that it would not be man enough to hold the ground. So, in order to retard its dragging process, we shackled on every conceivable heavy object – tank strops, tank-door extensions, everything but the galley stove: all were allowed to slide down the cable to the sea-bed as added weight. And still the gale blew with every-increasing intensity.

By now our engines had been at 'full ahead' for more time than was healthy and, having in mind that we had yet to beach, discharge our load and then get back to Portland, it became prudent to look for some other means of staying off this terrible lee shore.

Closing a liberty ship, we persuaded her to pass down a six-inch grass rope, which we manhandled aboard and made into a bridle and, after much adjusting, we finally rang down, 'Finished with main engines.'

Still on the bridge, exposed to all that this abominable gale could throw at us, we braced ourselves against the rail and got what sleep we could standing up.

This bliss was too good to last. Within the hour the continual jolting of the waves had chaffed the grass rope to shreds and we were adrift once more and trying to fight our way out of the world's most over-populated anchorage. Would this screaming gale never abate? And would the glass never start to rise?

The feeling of weariness in some of the crew was by now obvious: they were cold and wet, sleepless and unwashed, after three days and nights of this struggle – and the glass showed no sign of rising.

I was instructed to prepare the craft for beaching!

I could not believe that I had heard such an order!, I questioned it:

'Beach her with a full load of vehicles, in this weather, on a lee shore, while we have both main engines capable of full power and with fuel in our tanks?'

The order seemed incredible to me – but it was repeated. 'Beach her in these conditions and we'll lose half our crew,' I said. 'Let's get back out into deep water for as long as we have fuel in our tanks. If you still insist on beaching, you could be court-martialled!'

The glass began to rise at last, the sun came out and finally we disgorged our load on the littered beaches.

We steamed for home in calm waters and on the way the CO

made out his report, a report that won him an accelerated second ring and an Admiral's Special Order of the Day:

4 July 1944

The following Special Order of the Day has been made by Flag Officer in Charge, Portland.

(1) I wish to commend the officers and men of LCT 628 for their good work in keeping their ship off the far shore for three days in the face of very adverse weather.

(2) The initiative of the Commanding Officer in deciding to stay at sea is particularly commendable.

(3) LCT 628 left Portland Harbour in convoy but on arrival at the far shore encountered weather so severe that it was impossible to beach.

(4) The stern anchor was lost and the bow anchor too light to hold the ship, the weather was also too bad to allow of LCT 628 making fast to the stern of other ships and several hawsers were parted in an endeavour to do so.

(5) Notwithstanding these difficulties LCT 628 was kept in operation and finally succeeded, when the weather had abated, in landing her load of US Army trucks on the shore.

G. T. C. P. Swabey,
Rear Admiral,
Flag Officer In Charge

Chapter Seventeen

'For Christ's Sake, Amen'

Loaded with American General Grant tanks, we pulled off the hard at Portland and went to a bouy to await instructions. During the afternoon a heavy rainsquall swept across the harbour, and later in the evening, when a north-west wind began to dry the deck plates, what we thought were a dog's pawmarks were seen on the iron deck.

I asked the coxswain if any member of the crew had brought a dog aboard. He answered, 'No, sir.'

At 2055 the quartermaster reported to the wardroom that it was 'five minutes to rounds, sir'. I got my cap and prepared to make the last inspection of the day. The final duty was to go to the wheelhouse and enter in the log the barometer readings. As we opened the door, a dog-like animal flashed past us and out into the night. As it was now quite dark, we decided that the matter would have to wait until daylight.

Before daylight next morning the coxswain reported that seaman Bates had gone to the heads (lavatory), only to find it occupied by a fox.

We sailed an hour or so later, and until we beached at Omaha some twenty-four hours later, we put down all kinds of food to sustain our visitor.

On this occasion, we beached at high water and a falling tide left us high and dry. A sharp watch was kept as each tank left, and although a thorough inspection was made of the ship, no sign of a fox was seen. Just how it had joined us, or how it left, was a complete mystery.

We assumed that somewhere in the Dorset countryside the vehicles had camped overnight, and the fox had entered one of them, possibly searching for food, only to find itself aboard ship *en route* for Normandy.

The strain of constantly flogging back to the beaches began to tell on both ship and crew, for the only respite came on the occasions when we beached on the far shore.

Our constant battle with the elements had also begun to show. Our tank-decks were buckled, splits in the main deck were opening up in bad weather, and our bottom tanks had to be continually pumped out. One LCT had actually fallen apart in mid-Channel, but its honeycombed construction was so efficient that the stern half had towed the fore-end back home.

The summer was fast disappearing and we were aware of approaching September gales and that this break of the season would bring on winter gales.

The Army was now well on its way to Paris and, with the port of Cherbourg now captured, the pressure on us had begun to slacken – our purpose had been served and inevitably this meant our return to naval routine and discipline.

The craft had been run ragged and our engines were rough, the main structures were strained and buckled. The authorities thought it was time to bring us back into 'good order and naval discipline'.

They bore down on us – quartermasters in the 'rig of the day', no more prowling back from the beaches alone, station-keeping at all times when at sea in company, the crew in the 'rig of the day' – and paint ship.

It was always recognised that, as soon as the main ports on the continent were opened, our craft work load would diminish.

We began to hear of whole squadrons being paid off and their ships laid up, and officers and their crews being made ready for the Japanese campaign. Certainly the number of ships began to thin out. Those of us considered to be seaworthy continued to do trips to the beaches, but at reduced frequency.

Late in November, we were ordered to sail to the River Orwell to be paid off, and in near-gale conditions ran up-Channel, through Dover and on up to Harwich into the calm of the Orwell.

This river was full of craft in various stages of being paid off; already scores of them had been run up on the mud and looked very abandoned.

We began the tedious job of de-storing ship in bitter weather – snow lay thick on the ground and a biting east wind howled in over the mud-flats. After only one day of this, it seemed that we were considered the most seaworthy craft available and so were ordered to sail to the Scroby Sands, opposite Great Yarmouth, where we were to load a German two-man submarine which had gone aground there. The crew had been saved and now this prize was to be loaded and taken to Chatham.

At Chatham, we went under the big crane, where we lay for many days and were visited many times by all the 'brasshats', who, it seemed, came from all over to inspect the prize.

Just how it happened I can't remember, but Joe Sharpe, my old shipmate from *Syringa* days, found his way aboard and we 'tired the sun with talking, and sent him down the sky'.

Finally our prize was lifted out; with only a short passage back to the Orwell, we returned to de-store ship.

In stages the ship was stripped of all movable objects and each day brought our living conditions a stage nearer to purgatory.

All fuel having been pumped out days ago, we now had no generators running, so we had no heat. With the outside temperatures well below freezing, trying to sleep was impossible in this unheated iron box. Finally we were instructed to run her up on the mud. We set her up and drove her in at full speed on the top of the tide. We dropped the anchor as we went in, and for the last time beached her right up among the trees.

We walked off and left her high and dry and rusting, and with her we left a slice of our own lives; but we brought away with us memories of the most monumental invasion ever devised by man, of countless hours and days of training, of sea-keeping, of gales, of fog, of calm and, of course, of painting ship. So many memories! The memory of the American full colonel arriving on board with all his staff and in the wardroom unwrapping a parcel recently arrived from home. Among the many goodies was a packet of popcorn, which we had never seen in the uncooked state, so here is a full colonel asking for a bucket, then going into our galley, much to the consternation of the cook, and proceeding to cook a bucketful of popcorn.

He was so pro-British that we were amazed at his whole attitude. He was also very proficient with a .45 automatic and demonstrated this on the quarterdeck, with an exhibition of fast draw and shoot.

From the American sergeants, who kept liaison on the bridge with us, we learnt that they were getting exactly double our pay; in fact, they were sending home more than we earned altogether.

Then there was the American ship that carved away our guard-rails while we were at a buoy; their captain promptly sent his men to repair the damage with their own welding set. This little problem would have taken half an acre of paper, all in triplicate, plus a court of inquiry, in our Navy.

For a short while we were attached to a Royal Marine mess which was close at hand. There was much speculation as to our futures. We were restless with this shore-based life, especially after a whole year of such intense activity.

My appointment to take a command course soon arrived and I was on my way back to Troon as fast as my bags could be packed.

Arriving at Troon, after the long and tedious journey up from the south by train, I was met with the news that there had been an error, the course was full – would I go back on leave for ten days after which a further course would be starting?

As fed up as this particular journey had made me, there is nothing quite so re-energising as the news of a bit of unexpected leave. I was away to Glasgow just as fast as I could go, after a meal and a clean-up.

I seem to remember that by the time I had finished this course and joined my new command in Oban, I had done the Kings-Cross-to-Glasgow-and-back trip some four times in thirty days and had stood in packed corridors all the way on all eight journeys. We had been told upon commissioning that we were now entitled to first-class travel, but as there were so few first-class seats per train, we would probably have had to stand anyway.

Back at Troon and its classrooms, its endless rain – and our old friend the padre, who informed me that the war in Europe had officially ended.

The course at Troon was short but concentrated. We were now, it seemed, destined to take ships out to the Japanese campaign and this would mean an extension to our knowledge of coastal navigation, which had been sufficient to date and because all our seagoing had been in coastal waters.

There was no time to teach us the traditional celestral course; this would have taken nine months. So they taught us astronavigation (in *nine* days!) in the hope that long before we had to make an ocean passage we would have had time to compare our workings with that of our coastal experience on our way out to the Red Sea. From there on it was the deep-sea stuff.

Each morning, as always, began with Divisions and prayers, taken in HMS *Dinosaur* in front of the hotel building and from the top of the steps at the front entrance. The padre, with the commanding officer and all his staff, stood arrayed and impressive; there were the usual prayers, with of course the naval 'Oh Eternal Lord God, who alone spreadests out the Heavens', etc.

One of the padre's little touches each morning was that one of the officers on course had to end the proceedings with the Lord's Prayer. When my turn came I found this to be a rather irksome duty, but felt that I had made a reasonable job of it, until getting towards the end I must have galloped and in doing so managed to get the wrong intonation on the 'For Christ's sake, Amen.' I was severely reprimanded by the padre.

We slogged through the course, which was all about the use of the sextant, which, of course, needs the presence of the sun, moon and stars from which to obtain the necessary angles. Yet for the whole of the time that we were on the course the west of Scotland emptied on us its special brand of rain; we saw neither sun; moon nor stars for the whole of the time we were there.

So, to acquaint ourselves with the function of the sextant, we sat in the classroom and, using the electric light-bulb as the sun, brought it down, with the aid of the sextant, to the wainscot for a reading.

Troon was not a very good choice in which to be taught the use of a sextant!

During one of the lectures, the need to pay great attention to detail was being developed, and to bring this point fully to our attention the following story was told.

It would appear that, at the Admiralty in London, right from the earliest days of the war, a round-the-clock listening watch was kept on every radio wavelength. Each message picked up was recorded and the naval ratings employed in this highly skilled, if boring job, could after a short time recognise the operator at the sending end by the personal 'signature' that he unwittingly developed.

One such operator, somewhere in distant Germany, became known as 'Old long break F', because he dwelt slightly longer on the dash in the morse code for 'F' than for any other break in the alphabet.

So sophisticated had their methods become that they could predict that it was time for 'Old long break F' to go on leave, and sure enough his signature would vanish for the required seven or ten days. Then it would return again.

Our agents in Germany had established that these signals were originating from a German Army headquarters, and this was of great interest to our people. After many months of looking down the throat of 'Old long break F', his signature suddenly ceased. He was not due for leave yet – perhaps he had been killed?

Then a week or so later, his signature came up again, but as the bearing in question pointed to the Arctic region, this raised the question, what was a German operator doing in the Arctic?

A destroyer was sent northwards in order to pin-point the fix and its source. The answer came back: Spitzbergen!

We had to know just what a German operator was doing in Spitzbergen, so a small force of destroyers was sent to this Arctic island and there they found the Germans were not only shipping out the valuable fish-oil, but had set up a weather station on the top of the highest mountain.

We put a landing-party ashore, blew up the fish-oil containers, took prisoners and wrecked the coal-dumps.

So much for the need for all of us to pay attention to detail. The Navy seemed so sure that this method of teaching astronavigation would be sufficient for our needs that, without having had the chance to use a sextant for its proper purpose, we were deemed to have satisfied our examiners and were sent home to await our next appointments.

Once again the dreaded journey from Glasgow, depart 2120, arrive Kings Cross, London, at 0700 next morning, standing all the way. Then cross London, hopeful of catching the 0830 from Waterloo to Weymouth.

Before leaving Troon, we were advised that while at home awaiting our appointments we could productively use our time by making out our watch and quarter bill for LCTs, for these were the types of ship it was expected we would command.

Imagine my surprise, having carried out this chore, to be told by our local doctor, who just happened to be visiting an ancient aunt of my wife's, that my appointment would be to the much larger, and more important landing craft infantry (Large).

Now, these I knew to be senior lieutenants' commands and I was only a senior sub-lieutenant! Besides, how on earth would a local doctor be even aware of matters such as this? I put the matter out of my mind.

In the next post or so my appointment arrived. I was baffled, for in large, red letters at the top was the word 'Confidential'.

It was some time after the war had ended that I found out from the doctor the full implication of his involvement in my 'confidential' appointment, and how it all tied up with my being given this senior command, which led to an accelerated second ring for me – but more of that later.

My instructions were to report to Oban, in Scotland, and there take over the command of HMLCIL No. 11. These were shallow-draft vessels built in America and capable of taking 400 infantry-men into the beaches. Once again, to join her in Oban I had to stand in a corridor from Kings Cross to Glasgow overnight with all my baggage.

Is it any wonder that I have never considered taking a holiday in Scotland from that day to this?

Chapter Eighteen

Command

A series of trains finally deposited me with all my gear in Oban at 0600 and I made my way along to the naval offices. It was that kind of a morning, a morning to remember up there in the Highlands – marvellous. Visibility out over the islands seemed to go on for ever.

I felt just a little threadbare from the journey and needed a wash and a shave, with, if possible, a good breakfast. The person awake in the offices was the OOW. Making myself known to him, I looked around while he read my attachment papers.

He offered the opinion that there must have been a mistake (shades of having to do the journey back to London), as only senior lieutenants were appointed to this class of ship.

Perhaps, he suggested, I might like to find my way aboard one of the craft alongside, where I could scrounge a breakfast and get cleaned up; I could leave my baggage with him, and if I came back at around 0915 the flotilla commander would be available, the whole matter could be cleared up and I would no doubt be catching the 1030 back to London.

Suddenly, the only thing good about the morning was the weather. (There had been so few of these perfect mornings in the Scotland that I had come to know.)

Strolling along the jetty, it was a great pleasure to see No. 11 there alongside. After LCTs it was with some interest that I observed how well she was armed – and, for my own comfort, if I ever did take command of her, she had a high bridge, which meant that I would have my own cabin under it.

She looked very smart, as if time had already been spent on getting her ready for the long passage out east. Having served my apprenticeship in tank landing craft, I found the whole design of this American-built ship new and fascinating. We had all heard of the amenities that these ships boasted, and now – who knew? – I might get to command one.

At this juncture I introduced myself aboard No. 11, and over breakfast, with lots of cups of coffee, the outgoing CO confirmed that only senior lieutenants commanded these ships and, if I were to get command, I would be the only ship of the twelve in the flotilla with a 'subby' in command.

It was with some trepidation that I made my way back to the office at 0915 to hear my fate.

Matters in the office were in hand alright. The flotilla commander was already in touch with the Admiralty in London. He explained that he was sure that there had been some mistake, and again I was given the same reasons; it was all beginning to sound like a gramophone record to me.

Would I wait until 1000 hrs? By that time he felt sure that the matter would be cleared up, and I could still catch the 1030 train.

Promptly at 1000 I was called into the office to answer still a few more questions regarding my past – and would I wait again? By now it was well past 1030 and I had lost the train to London. Eventually I was asked into the office of a rather sheepish flotilla commander – mistake or not, I was to stay and carry out the appointment on my attachment paper.

That evening I dined with the commander and he tried to prise out of me more details of my past, but as it was only after the war had ended I learnt the full facts of the matter, all I could do was recite to him my progress from ordinary seaman to seaman, leading seaman, then to petty officer and coxswain, prior to my commissioning.

At this stage, I would have been better able to shed some light on this matter had a letter from My Lords Commissioners of the Admiralty, dated 5 March 1945, and sent to me at my home address, not been lost in the post.

A facsimile arrived some weeks after I was demobbed. My appointment to take over command was dated 23 July 1945:

Sir,

I am commanded by My Lord Commissioners of the Admiralty to inform you that they have had before them a report of your good services in the planning and execution of the operations for the invasion of Normandy, and I am to say that Their Lordships have noted with satisfaction the part you played in this great enterprise.

I am Sir,
Your Obedient Servant,
H. V. Markham
Sub-Lieutenant Herbert Gordon Francis Male RNVR

Next morning I took over command of LCI(L) 11, wondering what Lieutenant-Commander Lawson might say now.

I found that, being an American-built ship, all her papers were made out in the American idiom. Our own Navy had some odd ways of expressing itself, such as 'chambers china, wrens for the use of', but this was something quite different. Every item had to be signed for; washbasins, lavatory pans, bollard, anchors, ship's bell, boats, right down to the last washer. List after list appeared – I must have signed my name a thousand times that day.

The ship even sported a shower, with hot and cold running water, and a wardroom that was not just a steel box on the upper deck, as in LCTs.

The handbasin quite properly emptied into the sea via a pipe instead of into a receptacle which had to be emptied manually. There were wardrobes, chests of drawers, bookshelves and, most significantly, a telephone system to and from all parts of the ship.

Even more fortunate was the 'high bridge', one of the only two in the flotilla, providing that much-prized individual cabin under the bridge.

Not for this reason only were they prized, for on the long sea passages that were to follow the unfortunates in the 'low bridge' type were shipping great seas right into the top bridge, while we were just too tall for that.

My Number One – or as they are called in the Navy, 'Jimmy' – proudly took me over the ship. He was somewhat older than I and instinctively I felt that this irked him. On the top bridge, he went in great detail through all the equipment, some of which I found most impressive, for it reminded me of my passage home in the destroyer HMS *Inconstant*. To cap it all she had a gyro compass! – No wonder these were senior lieutenants' commands.

But all this time my eye kept wandering back to a rather splendid OOW's seat, on a very efficient swivel and well padded. This was a Yankee innovation and one of which I did not approve, but obviously it was the apple of his eye. I had to find a way to get rid of it, without causing too much aggravation or the 'new broom syndrome'.

My commanding officer in *Cocker* had been an ex-deep-sea man. 'It is too easy to fall asleep,' he used to warn me. 'When you are in charge of the bridge always move around, never stand in the same place too long, keep moving.' So the swivel chair had to go!

From my conversation with the surviving Asdic rating whom I had visited in hospital, the watchkeeping officer in *Cocker* when we were torpedoed had in fact been seated – against all the rules.

A day or so later, I prevailed upon the flotilla 'chippy' to fit duckboards to the top bridge. This, I felt, gave greater comfort to the feet in long watches; at the same time I saw to it that the swivel chair could no longer be accommodated. It was stowed in the after steering flat and forgotten. Forgotten, that was, by all except my 'Jimmy', who over the following days made it obvious that we were temperamentally unsuited to spend what might easily be a long overseas commission together. So he was removed.

In the days that followed, I was introduced to each CO in the flotilla. This is usually accomplished by the simple method of hoisting pennant 'Nine' at lunchtime – pennant nine is green and white and for the purposes of social gatherings is referred to as 'Gin and Lime'.

It began to appear that I was under some sort of 'approval' for being the new boy. Every dirty job seemed to come my way, like being sent to sea in gale conditions to find and tow in a sister ship, but it could have been my imagination.

We began to hear of a full-scale inspection, first of each individual ship, then a passing-out parade of the whole flotilla ashore.

Among so many other things that are the lot of a newly appointed CO, we had to prepare for these two inspections, added to which the whole ship had to be repainted.

To those who have experienced the painting of a ship, there is no need to describe the chaotic scenes that it can produce. Usually, just as all hands are happily slapping on the paint, a signal comes to move ship. In our case, we were ordered to proceed to the measured mile to do our speed and engine trials.

These ships are powered by American twin diesels of the kind that cannot be reversed, but a rather sophisticated method of varying the pitch of the propellers is used to produce the power to go astern; the only problem was that, from ringing down for 'full astern', in the case of an emergency, there was an interminable delay while the engine was declutched and the revs reduced then re-engaged.

All this was new to me and, coming in from trials in full view of the whole flotilla, the new boy handling his ship for the first time was himself very much on trial.

But it occurred to me that, with twin screws, the problem was not that insurmountable, so it was arranged with the chief engineer that at all times, when coming alongside, the outboard engine would be stopped and clutched into 'astern' position – so that if I found myself in trouble I could get immediate 'astern' on one shaft.

I made the kind of alongside that comes straight out of the textbook – the gods were with me that day.

Later in the week it was decided that, for the passage out east, I should carry all the flotilla engineering staff, so that in the case of breakdowns (and there were many) I should go alongside, deposit the engineers then take the stricken ship in tow until repairs were completed.

This onerous job had been awarded me firstly because I was junior in rank to all other COs and, secondly, because, as a petty officer in minesweepers, I probably had more experience of towing than any officer present.

For the next few days we berthed alongside and a whole gamut of engineering stores were brought aboard, mostly heavy engine parts, drums of oil and toolkits. All this had to be lashed and stowed for a long sea passage and the addition of further engineering staff meant even more cramped living conditions for the crew.

A hastily erected cabin in one of the spaces where we would normally have carried infantry was prepared for the engineer officer. All this meant great activity everywhere in the ship – our newly painted ship; now it would have to be done over again if we were to pass the pending inspection.

The hills beyond Oban looked inviting, but we were running late and, as much as we would have liked to walk in them, we had to be content with a stroll along the front each evening after dinner.

The provisional sailing date was fixed and the thought of this put a spur into our work. Many of the officers were finding it difficult to purchase the requisite tropical kit, having left it until they got to Oban, but so much of my petty officer's kit could easily be adapted – in most cases only the renewal of buttons was necessary – that I found I had clothing coupons to spare. With these I purchased a kilt and posted it home for my wife.

The inspection of the ship, by the base captain, was a bit of a worry but it all passed off quite well, and when it was over we wondered what all the fuss had been about.

All that now remained was the grand march-past and for Oban this was made into quite an event. From somewhere a Royal Marine band was raised and we made a passing fair show in the crowded streets of the small town.

We sailed for Plymouth in a freshening breeze and, forming up in line ahead, made our way out of the Firth of Lorne into a darkening sky.

South to the Island of Jura, then through the narrows of Islay, where of all places it came down thick of fog and we had to smell our way out of trouble. Now the long leg down to the Mull of Kintyre. By dawn it was blowing fresh and our station-keeping was the cause of many an irate signal from the squadron commander. The cause of this was put down to the fact that most of our quartermasters had been trained on the old ship's-wheel type of steering, but these, being American-built, had the quite unknown contact arm, rather like the ones on our old tramcars, and it was taking a great deal of practice to maintain correct station.

We made a comfortable ten knots during the night and with dawn were able to check our position. A new course was set for the Mull of Galloway and we ploughed on into quieter waters, finding our seamarks abeam, we set a new course for the Isle Of Man.

By now we had settled down to acceptable station-keeping; at least we were getting fewer irate signals, and with the sun in our faces the ship's company was rapidly shaking down to sea duties and watchkeeping.

We seemed to have acquired a good cook. The meals that were coming up were very good indeed for a small ship – but I expected complaints, there always are! It is surprising what being at sea does to men's appetites.

The second night at sea was quiet and moonlit, making the ever-irksome task of station-keeping a little less of a problem. We ploughed along with our engines humming a satisfactory tune and all the time appreciating the value of a gyro compass.

The characteristic of this type of compass is that it points to true North and not magnetic North. As all lines drawn on the chart must be True, no corrections are necessary to any bearings taken.

The coast of Wales went slipping by and the ship's company, both on and below deck, seemed to be getting used to the amenities of this American ship.

Our engines ran on smoothly and the weather seemed to be settling down to a fine spell. We exercised the ship's company in every conceivable evolution and found that, like all ship's companies, they moaned a lot but did their jobs well.

The coming dawn should bring us close to Land's End and then the last alteration of course into Plymouth.

Dawn broke fair and as the sun came up it was so calm that it was hard to believe that this could, in its worst moods, be a frightening area.

Breakfast was being enjoyed when a phone-call from the bridge alerted us to the fact that we were running into thick, cotton-wool fog!

On deck we streamed a fog buoy and cut our speed to 'slow', and the morning that had broken so fair was now a menace, as we were nearing the Longships lighthouse.

We cursed loudly and crept along, keeping the fog buoy of the ship ahead close to our port bow, a wearisome experience. As thick as the fog was at deck level, our topmast seemed to be in sunshine.

For fully three hours we crept along at slow speed, then as suddenly as it appeared the fog thinned out and disappeared – and there we were, far too close to the Longship rocks for comfort.

Without waiting for an order we each altered course away to port and safety.

With the crew at stations for entering harbour, we wound our way up the twisting river Tamar and made fast to No. 17 buoy, proceeding to water and store ship.

Our overboard discharge pipe was reported defective and we were told that it would be inadvisable to attempt an ocean passage with this problem, so at 0800 we slipped, and in thick fog proceeded down-river and into No. 4 basin for repairs.

The fog was really thick and the river full of traffic, but by smelling our way along we finally secured alongside the south wall of the basin.

Then began the task of pumping out forty tons of fuel in order to list the ship thirty degrees so that the offending pipe could be welded.

We lay all night at this alarming angle.

Chapter Nineteen

Deck Log

The following are excerpts from a diary kept at the time.

1 Sept 1945

Dull skies, full of rain, have to attend a conference at Granby Barracks – got soaked getting there. All usual formalities of a convoy conference, masses of information and paperwork. More than usual for me because I am towing ship.

Back aboard, slipped, and 'Being in all respects ready for sea' we proceeded in accordance with previous orders. Made complete hash of getting out of the basin – engines feel sluggish and not obeying telegraphs.

Before getting out to Drake's Island had to report port propeller fouled. Ordered to return and get services of a diver.

Propeller not foul, but the more complicated pitch control to propeller blades useless. This needs docking and is an engineering defect beyond my control. This explains my inability to turn short round in the basin.

2 *Sept*

Awaiting instructions to dry dock, defuelled down to nine tons, de-ammunitioned ship, all very tiresome. Chased up base engineer's office. Told to dock next day at 1500 – back alongside *Bradford* awaiting our time to dock.

Saw HMS *Inconstant* again, Phoned my wife and arranged for her to come to Torquay to stay with EO's wife – we can visit from Plymouth.

3 *Sept*

Lieutenant Lamb RN reported aboard for training! Made him navigating officer for the voyage – he is very keen and efficient, his last ship was HM cruiser. Singled up and docked at 1500 . . . dried out at 1900, caught train to Torquay – found Triss waiting.

4 *Sept*

Up at 0615, breakfast and away by bus to Plymouth, arrived at 0900, defects well in hand – it seems we need a whole new propeller shaft, a new one has to be brought down from Oban. All water and electricity turned off, crew has to use dockside 'heads', no hot meals while we are dry-docked.

Returning for divers' report was a wise decision. The sophisticated mechanism to vary the pitch of the propeller is at fault, no wonder I made such a hash of getting out of the basin – back again to Torquay.

5 *Sept*

Brought EO's daughter back aboard with us for the day, and to take home a kitten, of which we have eight to chose from. Work a little behind due to a small grub screw, which has to be brought from Staines. After frantic panic we undocked and did basin trails – back alongside the *Bradford*.

Returned to Torquay for the last time.

6 *Sept*

Arrived back in Plymouth, Lieut. Lamb moved ship to oil berth and in doing so had holed her above the water line – had plate welded on.

Re-store ship, re-ammunition ship, re-fuel. A Petty Officer Mosely was brought aboard under escort, he is to take passage to Malta. Slipped at 1500, proceeded out of harbour, wind fresh and sky overcast – making good speed, rolling comfortably. Put clocks back one hour – Eddystone lighthouse abeam, set course for Ushant.

7 Sept

Am taking the standing 'afternoon and middle' watches, the middle is known in the Navy as the 'graveyard' watch – should pick up Ushant light around 0130 on my watch, due to haze this is doubtful. Plenty of shipping but no Ushant light – making ten knots. Morning broke clear and bright, continuing to make good progress. Sighted large fishing vessel under canvas. Logged 251 miles for the first twenty-four hours – should sight Cape Finnesterre at noon tomorrow.

8 Sept

Ahead of schedule, weather boisterous with lumpy seas, rolling steadily. 1050 sighted Finnesterre, now proceeding at twelve knots, wind fresh from the SW. This is indeed a frightening coast. Sinister Finnesterre, as the 'Jimmy' said. With the dreaded Bay of Biscay behind us we heave a sigh of relief as this SW wind is now freshening.

9 Sept

Carried out gun practice, fired all small-arms, now running down the coast of Portugal, cliffs very high and menacing. Plenty of shipping, British Cable ship bound home. Now many Spanish trawlers, ship has plenty of motion, Lieut. Lamb not yet used to the motion of small ships and is very sick. Now the run down to Cape St Vincent.

10 Sept

Entered the Straits of Gibraltar with a fierce breeze on our port bow, shouldering heavy seas awkwardly, decks awash – bright sunshine and clear skies – as yet our engines haven't whimpered in four days at 425 revs. Night calm, got several fixes from Cape St Vincent. Our main trouble is fresh water, which in only four days we have had to ration – shall have to arrange for added water-tanks when we sail across the Indian Ocean. Normally our compliment is twenty-six, including engineering staff, am now carrying forty-one.

11 Sept

Arrived Gibraltar, secured alongside at 2230 – some difficulty in finding correct berth.

12 Sept

Hive of activity today, water ship and store ship, decide not to pipe leave until all departments were ready for sea. To Paymaster for pay. Pipes leave 'to watch and part'. Enjoyed first run ashore in Gib; bought small gift and posted it home. Saw ceremony of the 'Keys' in the main square. A welcome addition to our diet were the bananas, melons, oranges, grapes, nuts and figs that we could buy. All hands aboard in a merry state – but no trouble.

13 Sept

Dense fog delayed sailing until 1100 – minor engine trouble, slipped and proceeded through 'C' and 'D' gates at 'full-ahead together'. Set course, made ten knots – weather fine, sea slight. Sunbathed on top bridge all the afternoon watch – no risk of enemy action, my first experience of this state of affairs. Off Oran at dawn.

14 Sept

Ran on at usual speed, the breeze has some weight in it now, may mean too much come sunset. Began painting out 'heads' and bathrooms, breeze freshened to gale, spent uncomfortable night pounding heavily into head seas – had to slow, jogged along.

15 Sept

Still very boisterous, sky clear, but heavy deep seas, making only four knots. Our ETA will be delayed at Malta – no sign of wind abating, in for another uncomfortable night – not getting much sleep. Remembered 'Monty's' much used remark (from *Syringa* days): 'All spare time spent at sea not in sleep is time wasted.'

16 Sept

0400, wind moderated, morning bright and clear, sea calmed during the day.

17 Sept

Hectic night off Pantelleria, fixed ship seven miles off lighthouse, lovely dawn, sea calm. Island of Gozo came up at 0730 – ran on and entered Sliema at 1210. After much delay received berthing instructions, finally picked up buoy abeam of hospital ship *Main*. Went ashore and found Capt. and Mrs Bray, old friends of my wife's.

18 Sept

Major defect needed slipping. Frantic activity, had at last caught up with squadron. Told to prepare for Vice-Admiral's inspection, so it's scrub and paint ship again. Met Ernie Woods – he is seconded out here from Portland dockyard.

19 Sept

In boiling heat held a squadron rehearsal for the coming Vice-Admiral's inspection – Royal Marine band from HMS *Norfolk*.

20 Sept

The BIG day! This is Malta's first big postwar naval parade. In sweltering heat on the hard sand at Taxbiex, 'Baker' Squadron was inspected by Vice-Admiral Sir Frederick Dalrymple Hamilton. His last command was HMS *Rodney* and he was present at the sinking of the *Bismark*. He made a great impression on us all, tall and very jocular. Later in the day defuelled and slipped at 'Phonecia'. Had the whole family of Brays aboard for lunch.

Dinner with Ernie Woods and friend back aboard at midnight.
21 Sept

Attended defaulters of the PO brought aboard at Plymouth, he was charged with 'violently resisting arrest' – he got sixty days in the glasshouse.

Capt. Bray came aboard – took 'Jimmy', 'Navvie' and me all around the island in an Army jeep, stopping at Rabat – bought a tablecloth to send home, much squalor in the villages.
22 Sept

Usual mess while slipped, no lighting, no water, paint everywhere. Am giving the lads all the leave I can – they seem to be making pigs of themselves with the cheap wine ashore. We take advantage of all the fresh fruit available.
23 Sept

Sunday routine – quiet day – dinner ashore with the Brays.
24 Sept

'Engines', 'Navvie' and self spent the afternoon out in a jeep with Capt. Bray. Medina Cathedral – amazed at the fabulous riches in the cathedral – and the destitution outside. Quiet night aboard.
25 Sept

Unslipped at 0900, proceeded to refuel at oil jetty. Dressed in No. 5's and attended convoy conference. Having made the passage from Plymouth to Malta unaccompanied, it will be a new experience to be in squadron formation.

Decided that as Capt. Bray and family had been so accommodating we should have the family aboard for dinner. This proved to be a great success, as food has not been too plentiful here on the island – bade them goodbye at 2330.
26 Sept

Left Malta on passage for Port Said

Hands called at 0600, clean ship and secure for sea, Ernie Woods aboard for early breakfast and to say goodbye. Posted letter to Harold Saunders, an old Portland buddy, he is quartermaster-sargeant in a West African regiment. By posting this letter I hope to meet him in the Canal Zone. Slipped at 0900, made way out of Sliema harbour, wind freshening – ran on into full gale conditions, rolled sickeningly for the first four hours, then changed course and ran before the gale, yawing uncomfortably in the following seas. Continued all night in this state, but made good progress – do not expect to sight land for thirty-six hours.

27 Sept

Dawn brought clear skies, but no abatement in the wind – now running before heavy seas, averaging 10.5 knots. All awash on deck – no hot food today! Sky cloudy, unable to get a fix – running on DR (dead reckoning) now for twenty-six hours. 'Engines' looking rather green – he isn't missing hot food. Glass showing first signs of rising, this suggests better weather tomorrow.

28 Sept

Wind dropped to light airs during the night – still making 10.5 knots. By the end of the 'middle' it was moonlight and quiet, expect to sight land around dawn. Port of Derna came up, fixed ship two miles north of DR position. Running along the North African coast all day – many old and familiar places now coming up on the chart. Mid-afternoon abeam of Tobruk. I spent ten months running here from Alexandria under siege conditions and the last time I left Tobruk was as a survivor. Later in the evening, stopped the ship, piped the 'still' and paid a silent tribute to old shipmates as we passed over the resting-place of my old ship HMS *Cocker*. Truly an area of many memories.

29 Sept

Weather very unsettled, it is the break of the seasons, so this boisterous weather must be expected. From Malta the greater part of the passage has been heavy going, many of the crew are due demob, grumblings are being heard – discontent is now bubbling below the surface. With civvy street just around the corner, here we are sailing to Cochin on the southern tip of India and possibly on to Luzon in the Far East – who knows?

30 Sept

Arrived off Port Said, am last to enter, as usual, being towing ship, no pilot necessary as I had entered the port many times before – secured alongside Arsenal Basin at 1400. Crew eager to get ashore.

1 October 1945

Same old Port Said, full of smells and 'gilly gilly' men and shoeshine boys. Await with interest the return of the liberty-men, they will no doubt be loaded with leather handbags, dirty postcards, and some will be missing their paybooks. The first time ashore in Port Said is always a great adventure, but knowing what a 'soft touch' Jack is when he is ashore the 'gilly gilly' men will have a field day. Hot, but not too hot. Had roast quail for dinner ashore, very disappointing, so small and so full of bones.

2 Oct

Storing ship is the main consideration, for civilisation ends here as far as stores are concerned. Made use of some of my 'old contacts' from way-back days – new fans and all kinds of fishing tackle – must keep the crew happy somehow. They do seem to accommodate small ships here, or is it the good offices of my old friend Billy Gilbert still operating?

Very hot and dry as usual, pestered by shoeshine boys, sellers of leather handbags, used the word 'Yalla' and even enjoyed using it, having done so many times in days past. Dinner in the Officers Club – really enjoyed this, after ship's cooking.

3 Oct

Pay Day – what a performance! As usual, the pay office was right out of town and, after paying our three ships' companies, the bank went broke. We had to return in the afternoon – eventually managed to pay ships company at 1600 and piped leave to the watch. Went ashore and walked again through the famous Simeon Artz emporium, bought present to take home.

4 Oct

Left Port Said and passed down the Suez Canal.

Hands shaken at 0530, slipped and proceeded in darkness, entered Canal, quite an experience conning a ship eighty miles in a straight line to Kabrit in the Great Bitter Lake.

All very interesting, but a constant eye has to be kept on the steering, especially when passing another ship – this is only permitted among small ships. Hot but making just a bit of breeze. Secured at Kabrit at 1630. Immediately received a signal from Harold Saunders, it seems he is only seven miles away.

5 Oct

Heat now overpowering, stores and water unobtainable, working tropical routine, up at 0500, work in the cool of the morning, finish at noon.

Swam all afternoon and tried to keep the flies away. Ashore to meet Harold, bathe together in the lake and return aboard for a late tea. Harold had to return to his unit but arranged to meet again on Monday.

6 Oct

Began painting out all the alleyways a lighter colour and it really is a great success; all hands got stuck in and the job was finished by noon.

Wireman Davies caused himself to be a great nuisance by coming aboard drunk, he decided to take a swim and nearly drowned. It appears that he took neat rum ashore – that and the heat had caused the problem. Found it necessary to water everyone's rum. This is the most dire punishment for the rum-drinkers, consequently they are most displeased with Davies.

7 Oct

Sunday routine, only necessary jobs are carried out. Church party ashore in No. 5's. Pipe down after dinner 'All hands to bathe and skylark'.

Very large tanker, *San Veronica*, passed, bound home.

8 Oct

Phoned Harold, expect him aboard later in the day. More painting on the upper deck and crew space. Huge liners go bowling by all loaded with troops bound home. My demob group is twenty-six, so have a little time to wait. Hot and very sticky. Harold aboard – we talk over old times and play Monopoly well into the night – he decides to overnight with us.

9 Oct

The 'Jimmy' and 'Engines' off to Cairo at 0630 for two days. At 0900 I leave with Harold for his unit in Fayad. Spent most enjoyable day with the Army. His unit are all West Africans – very amusing! They are a labour unit and some of their customs are hilarious. Late night in the mess.

10 Oct

Shaken at 0700 by a huge black sergeant with a cup of tea, enormous breakfast followed, then watched Harold at work – in the heat of the desert. Finding it very hot here, miss the sea breezes if only for a day or so. By transport to the Canal and bathed again for an hour or so and talked of what we should do after our demob. Back aboard, to find a pile of signals needing my attention – so ends a few hours with the Army.

11th Oct

Day began with a conference on the trip so far, it lasted two hours and became a bit of a bore. Afternoon, Harold arrived with a lieut. from his unit, had early tea, but had to rush off to a party at HMS *Saunders*, for which I was detailed. All stood around and made polite conversation. Then a very good ENSA concert followed by a most enjoyable musical evening.

12 Oct

AB Inglis in the 'rattle' for sleeping on watch. At least he is honest and makes no excuses. Four letters from home, first since Plymouth.

We scrape and paint the dinghy and have rigged it to sail with the fin off of a barrage balloon – the idea is fine but the sailing is hopeless.

It is becoming increasingly difficult to live with a certain member of the wardroom – this is his first sea draft and he doesn't like it one little bit.

13 Oct

Saturday routine, did upper deck rounds at 1100, usual tour of inspection then 'pipe down'. Have seen no rain since we left Plymouth, now very hot and dry. Find myself reading poetry again, have done this on and off all the time in the *Andrew*.

14 Oct

Slipped and proceeded to Suez. This order came out of the blue and had no time to phone Harold before sailing. Arrived Suez late afternoon.

15 Oct

Had hoped to phone Harold today but it proved impossible. Ashore in Suez – what a fly-blown place. Came back to Port Ibrain and had tea in the NAAFI then an open-air cinema, quite good. Back aboard.

16 Oct

Last chance to top up on all stores and water. All ship's company that could be spared sent ashore for fresh food and what stores we can get, remainder clean ship and paint stanchions. Very hot during night. None of us will be too upset to be leaving Suez – it's a dump.

17 Oct

Leave Suez for Cochin (southern India) – (a three-week passage)

All hands called at 0600 hours, scrubbed down decks, secured for sea. We sail at 1600 for India. Hurriedly get a letter off home, then begin checking all gear required for ocean passage. Blistering hot at midday, gyro settled down – it requires to be started twenty-four hours prior to being used. Day dragged on, all mail away to *Saunders* for onward posting. 0345, shortened in at ten fathoms and awaited turn to get under way. Passed 218 (flotilla commander) and piped ship – took up station and proceeded at 'slow'. While only eighteen miles out took No. 9 in tow – not a good omen – we have 3,000 miles yet to go. Night cold, see rough, yawing badly.

18 Oct

Early this morning passed HMS *Victorious*, bound home; by Aldis she made 'Going the wrong way – the war is over'. Red Sea full of shipping, odd to be at sea with all ships showing so much lighting after being blacked-out for so long. Running before quite a sea and making 9½ knots.

It's a thousand-mile steam to get out of the Red Sea, desert both sides but sea islands in plenty at the far end. Handed over the watch to 'Jimmy' with instructions that 'nothing was coming up'. An hour later, my phone rang, I was called to the bridge – there fine on the port bow we had raised a light!

This was totally unexpected, and from long reference to the chart found that no light could come abeam until *noon* the next day. This light was 110 miles away. Checked position with other ships in company – they too were mystified.

This phenomenon, it seemed, when we consulted the *Red Sea Pilot*, was due to refraction, or the bending of rays of light, by the suspension of myriads of tiny specks of sand in the atmosphere. A kind of mirage, not uncommon when making passage in the Red Sea.

19 Oct

Fresh breeze all day, glad of some fresh air for a change, but the wind is hot. Convoy well bunched up and as 'arse-end charlie' found station-keeping easy. Stokers commence drawing Red Sea pay today and they will earn every penny of it (7d. per day). The large fridge in the messdeck shows signs of going on the blink, if this cannot be rectified will have to dump all fresh food overboard.

20 Oct

Heat increasing, can keep middle watch stripped to the waist and still drip with sweat – but the sudden drop in temperature at 0400 a.m. means that we need a duffle coat for the morning watch. All hands had bacon and eggs and tomato for breakfast just in case the fridge is going on the blink. AB Goodhead makes a fool of himself, having, after many warnings, had his 'mick' cut down – very sorry for himself later in the day. Had to dump all remaining food in the fridge overboard. Reported my situation to HQ ship.

21 Oct

Stood by to run on into Aden to replenish fresh supplies. All surprised at how quickly the food turned putrid after the fridge broke down.

22 Oct

Ordered to proceed at twelve knots into Aden to restock and be outside to rendezvous with squadron at appointed time. Broke away and proceeded as ordered. Sea now lumpy and at twelve knots am bouncing about quite a bit. Ploughed on all day at this speed.

23 Oct

Altered course at Perim Island at 2120 and, still at full speed in now calm waters, made Aden at 0710. Store party ashore – found everybody most accommodating – topped up with fresh water and were ordered to leave as soon as able. A welcome break for the crew, although no shore leave.

24 Oct

Rejoined convoy and took up station – by midnight am towing two craft and this is not an exercise! By now have had so much experience at picking up a tow that we have cast aside the Naval method and by polishing up our newly evolved technique could now cut down the time from sixty minutes to just ten.

The last time I came south in the Red Sea was as a passenger in the troopship *'Niew Amsterdam'* and that was some three years ago. Little did I think then that my next time here would be in command of my own ship, taking her across the Indian Ocean to Cochin, on its southern tip.

At a point about halfway across the Indian Ocean, I was called to the bridge around 2200. The 'Jimmy' explained that he was confused by a mass of individual flickering lights away on the port bow; whatever it was it bore no relation to any pattern that we could recognise as any of the usual lights carried by ships at sea. Lights that seemed to leap into flame and then die down immediately, almost as if someone was feeding a fire on the upper deck, and yet the whole armada was moving along at quite a pace.

This was indeed a puzzle, yet they seemed to be aware of our presence, for it was they who were avoiding us. Dotted all over, as far as could be seen, were scores of these ships. Only at dawn did we see that we were in the middle of the annual migration of dhows. These ships have been in this trade for hundreds of years.

The special lateen rig that these ships use was developed from the fact that they would be on the same tack for weeks on end, blowing from India and Arabia on the north-east monsoon winds to the east coast of Africa, where they would trade their goods, then with the money buy a return cargo and sail back the 3,000 miles before a south-west wind.

It seems that the Arabs had settlements in Africa some 700 years before the Portuguese came around the Cape in 1500. These settlements must have depended upon regular communication by sea and these Arab ships were their link with home.

Exactly when these seamen became aware of the seasonal change of the wind is not recorded – it is enough to say that these shipmasters have understood the seasonal change of wind and used this knowledge to make ocean passages in excess of 3,000 miles, and without a traditional compass, just the old lodestone.

In olden days, these dhows brought all kind of cargoes – dates, beads, dried fish, warm rugs – and traded them for ivory, cereals and human slaves, which they transported back to Arabia. After the end of slavery, they still sailed down to Mombasa and Lamu, bringing carpets, carved chests and a variety of other Arab trading goods. These they sold as best they could, returning home with mangrove poles, charcoal, grain, sugar and tea.

The many confusing lights that we observed were in fact open brazier fires, kept on deck firstly for cooking and warmth, then as a warning to other ships – no wonder we were confused, as no mention of this centuries-old habit could we find in any book.

These lateen-rigged dhows are, it is said, the most efficient sail plan of any of the world's sailing ships, providing they are used in the open sea and on a fair wind.

Dates were important to the dhows' economy, so much so that their displacement was not calculated by tons but by the number of boxes of dates they could carry.

We continued to sail through great numbers of these beautiful craft for most of the morning, fascinated by their simple yet lovely lines, and further intrigued by the lonely plank that stuck out some eight feet or so from the ornamented transome. We cogitated at some length on its purpose, until we saw an equally lonely Arab sailor inch his way backwards along planks to the very end. There, literally hanging on by his teeth, he defaecated! This, it seemed, was the open-air model. There were some ships, we noted, with a box-like contraption slung over the stern. This was dubbed the 'thunder box' by our 'Bunts' and was only used when female passengers were being carried.

The ship's company, being of the Muslim faith, would see that any such female was locked away in a small cabin for the whole of the voyage and only a very elderly member of the crew would be given the job of taking her food. She could only use the 'thunder box' after dark.

At prayer time, which is five times per day, the entire ship's company knelt facing east, while the ship, at not inconsiderable speed, would be ploughing on its course.

Vasco da Gama noted that, apart from the use of the lodestone, these intrepid Arab seamen had from the earliest times been in the forefront with their observations of the heavens.

The need for mangrove poles in Arabia is interesting. They are mainly used as tent poles. There is no indigenous source of tent-pole wood in the whole of Arabia, so these tough mangrove poles have been transported across the Indian Ocean for centuries – the Arabs export their dates in return for them.

25 Oct

Still have two craft in tow, but at 1030, with repairs completed, we slipped, recovered engineer's staff and took up escort on port column as ordered. Proceeded at 'slow' all the forenoon – painful to watch the log reading advance so slowly, averaging only four-and-a-half knots against the twelve to Aden. Ordered to take up and tow No. 224 – EO's staff put aboard – towing.

26 Oct

Quiet night towing – no nasty signals – no station-keeping, just jogging along, sea calm as glass. Lovely 'middle', large plate of chips, mug of coffee – just minding our own business. At dawn 224 was able to steam under her own power, slipped and regained EO's staff.

Half an hour later took up and towed No. 302. Have got this towing lark off to a fine art now, 'Jimmy' and crew know exactly what to do – with just hand-signals from the bridge.

27 Oct

Quiet day, making better progress. After a peaceful 'middle' the wind freshened – now rolling violently, had to pass a spare part across to No. 163 by line – too risky to go alongside.

28 Oct

Sunday routine, now blowing hard, heavy cloud, no hot food, galley awash.

29 Oct

Very boisterous night – am sleeping heavily, which is most unusual for me. Five of the crew complain of severe headaches, blame is laid on the mepacrine tablets that we are taking in lieu of quinine, which is no longer available. Condition clears up of its own accord after a few days of medication. Can easily tell those of the crew who are carrying out the daily dose of mepacrine as ordered – the whites of their eyes have all gone yellow. Heavy downpour at 1800, sea calm – still heavy clouds.

30 Oct

Glass rising – cleared lower deck and gave the crew a talking-to – some homesickness is beginning to show and seventeen days in a small vessel at sea in over-cramped conditions, and for many the first time away from home for any length of time, is probably the cause of the trouble.

'Engines' is a contributory factor also; instead of showing an example he moans at the slightest provocation. Five-and-a-half years in the Navy and this is his first seagoing ship.

31 Oct

Nasty swell from the SE – she wallows and slides. Off watch, have monthly payments to do, weekly returns, etc. – payment is now a huge job of paperwork – getting low on fresh food, beans now figure largely on the menu – 'Engines' complains! Cook has been making bread for some days now with dehydrated yeast, haven't yet been able to convince the crew that what he is turning out is edible! Shall be glad to get to Cochin, if only to get fresh bread.

1 Nov

This should be our last full day at sea – only one more 'middle' then shall have all 'night in' (my bunk). 3,000 miles non-stop in these small craft is no mean feat. Our engines have done much more than that, for towing adds to the strain – and sometimes we had two ships in tow, employed crew chipping decks, on the shady side, so at the moment she looks like a pigsty. ETA Cochin 1000 tomorrow.

2 Nov

Arrived Cochin, Southern India

Seventeen-day passage, squadron entered, we remain outside until the last ship is inside – just in case any towing was necessary. Observed first sea-snake, a yellow brute with black stripes – sharks also. Entered, finally secured to a 'dolphin' in a very obscure part of the harbour, a forlorn expanse of water.

3 Nov

Attended conference of all commanding officers aboard HQ ship; a long inquest ensued. A very detailed log had been kept by the squadron commander of every signal sent to every ship and comments on with what alacrity these signals had been complied with followed. Our towing efforts had been observed and compli-mented upon. Each officer was now told his demob number: mine was twenty-six. Each of us requested to ignore our demob and asked to continue with the squadron on up to Luzon. It seems that, these being American-built ships, they have to be returned to America. From Luzon, in the Philippines, across the Pacific to San Francisco, returning home by crossing America and then the Atlantic. Given twenty-four hours to think about it.

Squadron commander informed me that I had been accelerated to Lieutenant.

4 Nov

Informed squadron commander that I intended to take my demob, for it seemed to me that, with the amount of towing already done, to continue for a further 10,000 miles was out of the question. Some twenty other officers had agreed with me. Was asked to reconsider, but felt that after six years at war I had drawn on my good-luck account too much – and we were entering the typhoon season.

Much later I learnt that our flotilla was caught in a typhoon and two ships were lost; mine survived the battering.

5 Nov

The humidity of this place is killing. We set a more severe tropical routine, up at 0430 in order to take advantage of the cool mornings. Ship needs more chipping and painting, this means that the foul red lead paint will find its way everywhere. The boys, with the exception of 'big Brown', get stuck in (Brown has always been a skiver), so all officers help with the painting I ask 'Jimmy' to see that Brown is put to work on the same scaffolding as me. As we have to lower the scaffolding together he has to keep up with me – after a whole day of this he calls a truce!

6 Nov

Pay Day, manage to keep ship's company painting until the last minute. Pipe leave at 1400 – not much fear of any trouble here, only three cans of beer per week per person. Went shopping in Ernaculam, bought some local craft as presents. Back aboard at 1700 with a bag of prawns, cook makes a fine job of these and we have a real spread in the wardroom with the newly arrived bread.

7 Nov

Our mail, or the lack of it, is the big problem now. It seems that a typhoon is raging up the coast – this has delayed our mail as no aircraft can take off. This is the 'little monsoon' season. Every evening, without fail, at around 1800 we get a downpour of tropical rain accompanied by brilliant lightning; by midnight all is dry again.

8 Nov

'Jimmy' has packed all his gear ready for his demob; being a South African he has different procedures than we have. Instructed to pack all our gear and be at twenty-four hours' notice for our demob.

A further fourteen days elapsed before I was relieved of command.

Most of the upper works now completed – she is looking good.

9 Nov

Slipped and proceeded to a more convenient berth. Trevor Wiren aboard, stayed to tea, played Monopoly, then to a miniature picture show aboard 130 – helped to pass an otherwise long, wet evening.

10 Nov

Carried on painting, Pete ashore most of the morning attending to his demob papers, instructed to pump all fresh water overboard and replenish with fresh supply from *Sulphur Bluff*, rain again tonight – it cools the place off for the morning – then it's back to the old humidity again.

11 Nov

Telegram from home informed me that I had become a father, Celia Ann arrived 5 Nov 1945. Wardroom full of people all day drinking to her health.

12 Nov

End of painting ship in sight. I wonder just how many times in the last six years I had helped to paint ship, and, if put into one large paint-pot, how large a container it would have to be to hold all the Admiralty grey paint that had been slapped on. Humidity still very high, very little to go ashore for.

14 Nov

Final touching-up today for the flotilla officer's inspection, above and below decks – generous in his praise, especially for the white enamel. Inferred that it would be another week before we could expect to leave the squadron, flotilla officer piped ashore.

15 Nov

Tons of mail arrived today. Being so long without, I piped a 'make and mend' so that the crew could catch up with things at home.

16 Nov

After being so busy painting ship it is difficult to find the lads enough work to do, everything is spick and span. Spent most of afternoon and all my money in the NAAFI gift shop.

17 Nov

My relief arrived aboard today, began immediately the task of handing over – this will take a few days, as it is now confirmed that these ships are to be sailed up to Luzon and the on to the USA. Every inventory will have to be spot on, every article checked – all confidential books signed for, all stores, all food, both fresh and emergency, deck watches, binoculars, loaned clothing, wash-handbasins, lavatory pans – most of this seemed so unnecessary, as the units in question were bolted or welded down.

After all this I could begin to collect and stow all my own gear. It really is surprising how much can be collected – the ships 'chippy,' seeing my problem, made me a fine steaming trunk (a large trunk 'not wanted on voyage') for all my books.

Invited to dinner aboard FO's ship. This I suspect is a farewell 'do', not really my cup of tea, but all went well. He went out of his way to remind me of his doubts in Oban, but felt that his recommendation for my second ring more than made up for this.

His end-of-six-months report contained the following: 'He has conducted himself entirely to my satisfaction. A keen, efficient and conscientious officer who will be missed from the Flotilla. Archibald Hutton, Lieutenant-Commander RNVR'

18 Nov

Sunday routine. After today I shall be living ashore, just coming aboard daily to carry on with the take-over. Have not yet officially handed over command. It's rather nice to be piped aboard every morning and again in the evening to be piped ashore.

19 Nov

My last full day in command. I hand over at noon tomorrow. Some of the crew have been drafted to other ships. Have orders to have all my baggage aboard No. 285 by noon tomorrow. It seems that we are to take passage up to Bombay in one of the spare craft.

20 Nov

All goodbyes now said, final handover took place at noon. Some twenty officers aboard No. 285 will make it a very crowded passage. Slip at 1700 and steam right through the squadron. As we pass each ship we are piped and then sent off with a rousing cheer, at the last ship in line a bugle sounds the 'Still', we all salute, then the 'Carry on' from this lonely bugle, and we sail away into the sunset.

21 Nov

Weather good, steaming at ten knots for four days and nights will get us to Bombay. This overcrowding means that not only do we share the watches but the spartan conditions as well; watch-keeping between twenty of us makes life a doddle. Mealtimes are a bit of a squeeze, we mostly stand around eating.

22 Nov

I find that by getting up at 0600 breakfast is much more leisurely and there is elbow-room to wash and shave in comfort. Saw sunrise and a little later observed Sun, Moon and Star in the sky at the same time.

23 Nov

While these ships are designed to take 400 troops into the beaches, the possibility of that number of men spending four days aboard, based on our experience, is quite appalling, and this is not without precedent, as we kept our troops aboard for three days, plus the passages to the Normandy beaches, in the D-Day assault.

24 Nov

Up at dawn, bathed in a bucket, washed and shaved, Bombay is just around the corner. Sailed into this harbour – full of some of the world's biggest liners. The sight of all these ships gives us hope of a quick passage home.

Humped our baggage to HMS *Briganza*. Here we were met with the saddening news that we would not be getting a passage home until January. Moved out to a transit camp at Chembur, this is some fifteen miles out of Bombay – no routine – no duties. Food very good and plenty of transport into Bombay.

Many days have now to be spent kicking our heels in these very pleasant surroundings while we await passage home and demobilisation.

We have individual cabins which have concrete dividing walls and just rattan blinds back and front. There are Indian servants in plenty, due to their caste system – it seems that the chap who fills your bath isn't allowed to pull the plug out to empty it, and so it goes on.

Most evenings we have a concert if only of gramophone records.

Up at 0600 each morning, it's all rather cool with great flocks of parrots in their brilliant colours in the trees.

Some of us go for a run before breakfast every morning, then shower and shave. While this was to become a pleasant and leisurely period in our lives it was also anti-climatical when compared with the lives we had lead during the last six years, and after only a few days a restlessness began to overtake us.

The war was over and we were still many thousands of miles away from home, our demob number had come up and we were impatient to get on with our lives in civvy street.

We were all made honorary members of the Cricket Club of India, where we could watch good cricket, enjoy fine food, swim in the large pool and get away from the crowded streets so packed with humanity. It was here they brought some of our prisoners-of-war who had survived the building of the infamous Burma Railway – we were all so shocked to see face-to-face man's inhumanity to man.

It made all my complaints of life in our troopships rather trivial. It seemed that there was some kind of election in the offing, crowds the like of which I had never seen before packed the streets, all yelling, gesticulating and waving banners. Ugly scenes developed and we were glad to get back into the peace of our camp at Chembur.

Gramophone concert in the wardroom all evening – very quiet, warm and enjoyable.

No end to the selection of food for breakfast – a meal that I have always enjoyed – then a long walk in the warm sunshine out over the golf course chatting with contemporaries about the future, sat watching hordes of parrots in the trees, the flashes of colour and the squawking they produce is beyond our comprehension when compared with the sparrows back home.

It is best to be back before lunch as it gets very hot and sticky. We are served a lot of sweet potatoes with our meals, these are new to us, rather like roast chestnuts, but we find that the novelty quickly wears of and we tire of this tropical dish. Table tennis tournament all afternoon – can't get used to this 'no routine, no duties' set-up.

Four of us decided to have a day shopping in Bombay. We had a bit of difficulty getting transport at first, but were soon on our way. The fifteen-mile journey was full of surprises, the biggest was to pass through a cremation ceremony taking place at the edge of the road. The body was laid out for all to see on the top of a pile of wood; the whole pile was then soaked in a kind of liquid butter and set fire.

All a bit strange to our eyes, as was the skinny buffalo used as draft animals, the high priests, in their saffron robes, and the untouchables, the lowest of all the castes.

Began our shopping in a Chinese shop, but as they only made shoes to order we passed on to a vast carpet shop. Came out having bought £80-worth of goods – I had not the slightest intention of buying when I went in, the salesmanship amazed me. Further, the proprietor, as I had little money on me and no cheque-book, allowed me to make out an ordinary piece of paper in the same way as a normal cheque and I brought the carpets away with me – how very trusting.

Lunch at a Chinese restaurant, my first experience of this sort of food – came away quite bloated and very satisfied. Thought we ought to walk this meal down, so not knowing the way we took off to walk to the Cricket Club of India. Eventually had to give up and hire a taxi – the excuse was that it was too hot. Sat watching cricket for an hour, then decided to have tea on the veranda. Who should be sitting there but Lieut. Tegg from *Folloit* days. Had a good old natter of the old days. Back aboard at 1900, early to bed.

29 Nov

Haven't been feeling too well these last few days, getting very little sleep, my teeth ache and one eye is very bloodshot, feels like a cold in my face. Spent all day in camp, tried to sleep in afternoon but only fitfully. So far no mail has caught up with us, probably sent straight back home from Cochin. Good cinema show tonight.

30 Nov

Feel greatly relieved this morning, ate a good breakfast and took a long walk on the golf course. Back in the mess, wrote long letter home – very hot and sticky now, taking many showers a day just to keep cool.

Evening show by ENSA – Gert and Daisy took over the whole of the second half – they worked jolly hard, but it just didn't seem to go over too well.

Later at the bar they were jolly good company.

1 Dec

Usual routine, good breakfast, shall miss all these eggs when we get home. Long meeting in the wardroom, we all voice our views that being shot out here fifteen miles away from the centre of things, we seem to be forgotten – nothing seems to be moving towards our going home. The meeting develops into a minor mutiny, promises were made to 'see if our departure could be hastened'.

4 Dec

Had to go to sick-bay this morning with a large sty on my eye, very depressing. This is the first time in the whole of the six years in the Navy that I have had to report sick. Would rather not have broken this record. At tea-time in the wardroom we all learnt that we were to sail home in the French liner *Île de France*. We had seen her at anchor when we came up from Cochin and had said then that the best would be good enough for us.

It would seem that our minor mutiny had done a bit of good, for at last we had a passage home in sight.

6 Dec

Went to *Briganza* for our sailing orders, hundreds of naval personnel milling about, all impatient to get home, long queues outside every office. After much standing about in the hot sun we get a draft number.

Found our way to the pay office, more standing around, paybooks are collected. This is a good sign – at last each of us is given £10 10s 0d advanced payment. This, we learn, however long it takes, will have to last us until we get home.

8 Dec

Packed all 'Not wanted on voyage' gear and saw it depart for the *Île de France*. At last it had begun – the long jaunt home via the Cape (she is too big to go through the Canal). Only one more day and then we join the much-sung of 'troopship that's leaving Bombay'.

Hastily vaccinated against smallpox. It seems that a case exists in the camp – with a bit of luck this jab will be the last of the many dozens that the Navy has given me over the last six years.

Escorting as we did when in *Cocker*, we sometimes ran into different ports quite regularly, and it didn't seem to matter what evidence we had of having been 'jabbed' a few days ago, we had to be done once again.

Suddenly England began to look a lot closer, although we had been warned by the authorities that in order to get this passage we must forgo our rights of a first-class passage and would be going steerage – that turned out to be forty of us to a dormitory, and four bunks high.

Sunday 9 Dec 1945

After a fine breakfast – little did we know that this was to be our last good breakfast until we got home – we embarked, after lots of bag-humping and queuing, sweating and moaning, aboard France's biggest liner.

Chapter Twenty

Bound For Old Blighty's Shore

Sun 9 Dec

Embarked to find the usual well-known discomforts of life in a troopship are present. We knowingly gave up our rights of a first-class passage – it appears that our places are taken by servicemen's wives and their families. Food is served cafeteria-style, then taken to our dormitory. However, we are at last homeward-bound and are quite prepared to put up with anything (and the authorities know this) for the next three, or four weeks.

Durban will be our first stop.

For the next two days our lives are ruled by the absolutely frantic preparations for sailing going on all around us. Tenders fly to and from the shore and it seems that the gaping hole in the side of the ship will never be able to take all the trunks, kitbags and other bundles that go pouring in.

Water-tankers ply in and out from the shore endlessly [despite which we were rationed for water long before we reached Durban].

Fuel oil is being pumped in from a clapped-out old rustbucket of a tanker and already the decks are untenable with hordes of people, and we still have 400 more women and children yet to come.

Meals are getting horribly like a cattle-market, and it is too hot to stay long on deck, the humidity is stifling and the only relief is to shower often, but of course we are banned from using the showers.

Perhaps when we get under way things will change.

12 Dec

The event of the day! We sail at 1130 hours and up to the very last moment people are still coming aboard, and still with large stacks of baggage.

1130 raised anchor, and it would seem as if all 8,000 troops and their wives are all singing 'They say there's a troopship that's just leaving Bombay'.

So, we leave the 'Gateway to India' singing the words we have all sung a hundred times during these last six years – never dreamed that we should actually take part in the event.

13 Dec

Making twenty knots in fine weather, decks full of people, finding a place to sit is impossible and meals are a shambles, but it is early days and hopefully it can only improve. The event of the day is boat drill. This ship was probably designed to carry 1,000 passengers in peacetime. We now have 8,000 aboard; the lifeboat capacity is for the 1,000 compliment – not the 8,000. A number of small rafts are available in an emergency.

The fun begins at the sounding of the emergency signal, when all 8,000 have to make their way to the upper deck and their own appointed lifeboat station. People who have to get to a lifeboat aft all seem to live forrard, and vice versa. The first boat-drill, like the first meal, was a shambles.

We get these drills every day – the only answer to avoid getting crushed on the stairways is to spend the twenty-four hours on deck – then you might have a chance.

14 Dec 1945
0500, ship stopped to bury a three-month-old-child. Dawn was much more cloudy than of late – this is a sign that we are nearing the 'line'.

To supplement our meals we find we have to spend a great deal of money in the canteen. Ship's run for the day: 513 miles.

15 Dec
Water supplies cut by half, don't know how the women and children can manage. Five small boys are found drunk in a cabin – this is hard to believe, as all troopships since 'Monty' took over are 'dry'.

16 Dec
Sunday routine, apart from crowded church services, not much different from any other day.

17 Dec
Second child buried at sea, sighted islands in the forenoon, kept them insight for some hours, scenery very tropical. Now steaming between islands at twenty-one knots, heavy rain-showers – upper deck cleared in no time.

Logging around 500 miles per day.

18 Dec
Sleeping with so many to a dormitory allows for little privacy and living out of a suitcase is always daunting. The early risers, of which I am one, at least get a bit of space in the washroom. Assuming that we enter and bunker at Durban, I have saved the greater part of my advanced pay to spend there, am however making a bit of a hole in this money in order to supplement the poor food with purchases from the canteen.

19 Dec
Looking forward to Durban. Those of us who have already sampled the hospitality of this port will know all the ropes; this is my third visit.

Picked up the coast at 1500 and ran down about ten miles offshore, huge thunderstorm passed to starboard, entered Durban Bay and dropped anchor at 2140 off the Bluff. Too late to enter. For the first time in six years we enjoy the illuminations of a large city from seaward.

20 Dec
All hands up and about at 0530, get washed and shaved before we enter harbour. Weighed at 0710 and made the risky entrance at twelve knots.

Found the well-loved 'Lady in White' still singing us in. Since war ended she has been brought to England as a guest of the nation and attended Buckingham Palace to be presented with a special Vellum of Honour for her voluntary services to the troops throughout the war.

Now began the panic to get ashore. We only have this one day – we pulled a fast one and got ashore at 0845.

The privations of troopship life are put well behind us, this one day ashore in Durban is worth it all. Same old Durban, generous, colourful, warm and very pro-British. Shopping for presents to take home with what money we have left. Had 'big eats' in a restaurant in West Street – but were not allowed to pay.

Brought aboard a gunny-sack full of fresh fruit. Have now only £1 left and that has to get me to England.

21 Dec

Departed Durban, now it's first westwards to the Cape then northwards all the way home, next stop Freetown. Crowds of South Africans throng the jetty shouting and cheering us out, and there again at the end of the jetty is our 'Lady in White', singing all the old favourites. There can't be a British serviceman who entered Durban during this period who hasn't retained the happiest memories of this generous city and its people.

Blowing hard outside. If this continues we shall have a bad time of it off Cape Agulhus.

22 Dec

Making the 'old girl' creak a bit this morning, heavy seas with blinding rain – not many appeared on deck this morning, or in the dining-hall.

Many folk are very sick and it still looks like blowing. At noon the upper deck is barred, so its only the stuffy dormitory left – and sleep.

These giant rollers are the effect of the meeting of the three oceans, the great Southern Ocean, the Indian and the Atlantic Oceans, and the 'Cape Agulhus roll' is spoken of with great respect by all seagoing men. Sun managed to break through but this only makes a wilder picture.

Around noon we 'miss our step' and hit a great sea – this great liner shudders! We learn later in the day that, although the lifeboat deck is all of fifty feet above the water-line, this great wave carried away a lifeboat. Most of us have served in small ships and are well used to their motion in heavy weather, but this monster is different! It's like being in a gigantic lift that keeps slowly sinking, or rising – we are used to much more violent motion.

23 Dec

Hove to off Cape Town to land a sick airman. In the lee of this lovely bay, probably the loveliest in the world, we can only dream of the delights of this city – no shore leave granted.

24 Dec

At sea, quite awful breakfast of bad sausage and mashed potato and a spoonful of marmalade with one slice of bread, after which we start a queue for the weekly 'nutty' ration, followed by boat-drill. Evening meal was a sort of mix-up of spaghetti and stew, with a fresh peach for dessert – and this is Christmas Eve!

25 Dec 1945

My third spent at sea and I hope the last. The authorities went to town today with the food – a quite stupendous Turkey dinner, with all the trimmings, a children's party in the lounge, music in the messhall.

Church party in the morning and all day long carol-singing on the upper deck. Fancy dress after dinner – 'Guns' in a very merry state, went all wet with just a bath towel around his middle and a towel turban on his head.

26 Dec (Boxing Day)

We suffered today from yesterday's extravagance – very poor meals. Many, including 'Guns', have a fat head; just how this amount of drink got aboard is a mystery. At last our turn comes for a picture show. Showing tonight is *Music for the Millions* – very applicable. Allowing for the bad talking and having to sit behind a large pillar, the evening passed quite satisfactorily.

27 Dec

Days hang heavily now. Have read all available books, exhausted all available conversation – spend most of the day sleeping, if not in our bunks then in any space we can find on the upper deck. Only a day or so now to Freetown, after that four or five more to Southampton. We all seem now to have passed into a state of numbness, a kind of anti-climax. Our deputations to the ship's office are met with the bland 'It's only a few more days now.'

28 Dec

Due in Freetown tomorrow. Very humid with heavy thunder-storms, heat below decks unbearable.

29 Dec

Off the gate at 0730 passed upstream to the main anchorage, dropped the hook. The usual swarms of 'bum' boats arrive and if we had any money left we would have bought their poor-quality fruit. Many of the natives now trading in the 'bum' boats had returned home from a spell in our Army and amused us greatly by standing up in their canoes and doing the most intricate rifle drills. Many had picked up the profanities that are part of a serviceman's life and in the most amusing ways used this vocabulary, usually quite out of context and all mixed up with a variety of dialects.

30 Dec

Raised anchor and proceeded to sea at 1530.

31 Dec Last day of 1945

At sea and heading for home. The food seemed to reach an all-time low today – everyone complains! Only a few more days now. Temperature has fallen today and the sky looks wintry. Ate the last of my 'nutty' ration today – was hoping to keep some for home.

1 Jan 1946

Weather now decidedly cooler and the sun is paler. Our Scottish friends work hard to keep up New Year's Day.

2 Jan

Today we were piped into our 'blues', most folk spend the day walking on deck to keep warm, until they tire, then they sleep. Long queues for a picture show in the afternoon. Wind strong to gale from the NW.

Several of the RNVR officers taking passage have spent five years seconded to the Royal Indian Navy and as such they have enjoyed a much higher rate of pay than we have; now, however, they find that they have let their 'blues' lapse, and are wandering around the ship trying to buy any secondhand suit of blue. The prices they are offering are quite astronomic – they just have to have suits in order to get through the demob procedures. With many others I had a No. 1 suit and a rather battered working suit – being down to my last £1 and with the prospect of a few more days yet to go with poor food and no 'nutty' as a supplement, I sold my working suit for considerably more than I paid three years ago. Money seemed to be of no concern to these people. Both parties were left well satisfied.

3 Jan

Very wild today, with threatening skies, must be in the area of the Bay of Biscay. Can now go to the canteen and restock the 'nutty', with a pile to take home as well. Suddenly, with the help of my old suit am feeling quite wealthy – could even afford to miss the mealtimes altogether.

4 Jan
Last full day at sea, a fresh NE wind to butt-up channel with. A chill in the air to warrant an overcoat. Engaged in making out all the usual customs forms and start packing all gear except toilet-bag and a towel.

5 Jan
Arrive Southampton, and the end of an era. Now begins the biggest panic ever. Customs officers see each of us in his mess. Then clean ship and reclaim own baggage. Travel warrants issued and by late afternoon we are at Southampton station. Finally caught train to Weymouth.

After only a few days at home my demob papers arrived. Living as I did on the south coast, I was instructed to report to Roseneath, in Scotland. Once again the dreaded overnight journey to Glasgow – surely this must be the last of the standing in corridors.

My final payment contained the princely sum of £80 – this I assumed was my much talked of 'prize money.' To complete my demob process I had to make my way to Guildford to collect my demob suit and hat.

To see my old mentor once again, I made a completely illegal detour by train to the Tyne and spent a very pleasant day with him at his home.

Then to Guildford for my 'bowler hat'.

Many years later, a cheque for 12s. 3d. arrived, informing me that I had been under-paid at my final checkout and this sum represented the 7d. per day 'Red Sea' money for the twenty-one days that had been overlooked from 1945.

It was comforting to know that every serviceman, throughout the whole period of hostilities, was by law guaranteed his old job back when he was finally demobbed. While home on foreign-service leave, I had been talking to my old boss, Mr W J Sansom, and he had volunteered the information that he had 'something better' in mind for me when that time arrived, but as I was in fact on my way out to the Japanese campaign 'that time' was far off.

With all formalities now complete and my demob leave ended, I was asked to present myself at the firm's headquarters in Bath at 10 a.m. for an interview with the board.

This I duly did on the appointed day, only to be told that the meeting had got off to a late start, would I come back at noon? Now with two hours to spare, I walked across the road, where in a large sunken garden a military band was playing. It was a hot day, so I hired a deckchair and must have fallen asleep – the next thing I knew was the band was playing 'The King', having completed their programme, and it was 1 o'clock!

The very least I should be at my first interview was punctual, yet already I was an hour late – full of apprehension I rushed to the office and was much relieved to be told that the board had gone to lunch and had not yet asked for me.I should now report back at 3 p.m.

It was nearer 4 p.m. when I was finally called for. After a short discussion I was offered a post as a representative. This rather pleased me, for in the past such jobs had not been filled from the floor of the shop; it would also keep me outdoors and that again was to my liking.

Above all people I would find it faintly ridiculous to be told that I was superstitious. Walking under ladders, breaking mirrors, having to touch wood, have held no terrors for me, yet for the whole of the time I was at sea I would, never knowingly, always have an odd sock in my locker.

I have not the slightest idea how or when this habit began. It could have been that, after a particularly frightening piece of action, I found one in the locker and from there on my subconscious took over.

I most certainly can't remember sitting down and deciding that from now on an odd sock would be my guardian angel! All I know is that I would go regularly to my locker and check it out, and if needs be, especially after I had returned from leave, I would go on deck and quietly drop a sock overboard, just to maintain the status quo.

My mother had a quite definite telepathic contact with me throughout the war. The night I was torpedoed east of Tobruk, some 2,500 miles away, she was sat in a chair in the bay window, saying that 'something had happened' to me.

On several occasions, when I arrived home quite unexpectedly, and well after midnight, she had placed a hotwater bottle in my bed, as if I was expected.

As in so many avenues of life, there are people we meet who have a great impact upon us. So it was with my naval stint – a man called Albert Watson, who became coxswain of HMS *Syringa*.

He was a fisherman from the Tyne with a stocky and powerful frame – a man of outstanding leadership qualities and a strength of character that was to impress itself upon me for the rest of my life.

Hard, but fair, he knew his job and demanded that you knew yours. It was not until I had passed out for leading seaman and had gone back to base that I learnt more of this much-respected man, from a man of his own calling.

Sitting around at 'stand easy', the talk, as always, drifted to what ships we had served in. On my mentioning *Syringa*, a Tynesider said, 'Then you must have known Albert Watson? He's not just a man, he's a man and a half.' Then out came the story of how, in a quite dreadful gale, Watson had gone overboard and saved a shipmate from drowning, with conditions at the time among the worst ever remembered on a coast that is known for its fearsome weather.

This act of bravery won for him a Lloyds Medal for life-saving at sea, which entitled him to wear a special blue ribbon on his right shoulder. But he chose not to wear this coveted decoration. For this same act of heroism, the then Prince of Wales presented him with an inscribed gold watch.

When I finally left *Syringa* as a leading seaman – the first rung on the seaman's ladder, a step that only his encouragement and endless help had steered me towards – I went on to become a petty officer coxswain.

It was the example that he had set that I used as a pattern in HMS *Cocker* – which led to a recommendation to sit for a commission and finally my own command, with an accelerated second ring. I owe Albert Watson a great deal.

After the war, we kept in touch – just Christmas cards, for he was no correspondent. We visited him in North Shields and both he and his wife came to Portland and stayed a day or so with us. Then, in January 1980, after we had failed to get the usual Christmas card, his nephew wrote to say that Albert had been housebound for many weeks after a serious operation on his stomach. I sat down and wrote him a long letter, reminding him of some of the days that we had lived through together and I especially thanked him for all his efforts on my behalf.

I reminded him of the time he disguised himself as a seaman and took stroke oar to help me pass my leading seaman's exam! I went on to say that it was his example and the standards that he had set that had done so much to help me to further promotion.

A month later a letter arrived informing me that he had died and that I would be proud to know that the substance of my letter had been read out to a massive congregation from the pulpit, a congregation of all the fishing skippers of the port, such was the respect in which Albert Watson was held.

On the occasion that we called at his home on the Tyne, he had just returned from a very successful fishing trip. My father and I breakfasted aboard with the crew, on freshly cooked fish, all piled high on a vast central platter from which we helped ourselves. This little story was to become my father's party-piece for years afterwards.

At our parting, the boot of the car was literally filled with turbot, plaice, sole, haddock, cod and boxes of kippers. We sped southwards dripping melting ice all the way down the A1. We had intended to stop at Oxford for the night but, having in mind the freshness of our cargo, we sped on homewards.

That was the last time I saw Albert, and so ended an association that I shall value for the rest of my life. I can still hear his broad Geordie accent and, when it was called for, the whiplash of his tongue.

One of my mentors when working in the quarry had served as a stoker in HMS *Iron Duke* in the First World War. He kept me fascinated with his stories of Jutland. Like many of the stokers that I served with in my war, he developed the capacity to overcome whatever fears he may have had of working in the bowels of the ship when under attack by adopting a fatalistic attitude towards being torpedoed.

Working below, in a maze of machinery and pipes, they stood very little chance of surviving and they knew it – my old mentor found great comfort in the fact that he had some twelve feet of coal-bunker between him and any torpedo. In my war, I actually knew a stoker who found a completely spurious comfort in standing on the stokehold plates in such a position that, right above him in the deckhead, some thirty feet away, was a circular ventilator.

He actually *believed* that if he were torpedoed, he would be blown straight up and out of this eighteen-inch hole. All of us, finding ourselves living with the daily dangers of war, took comfort in some superstition or other – mine was , of course, always to have that sock in my locker.

The Doctor Ricks Story

Some little time after war had ended, I was invited to a talk given by an ex-Fleet Air Arm pilot on his experiences during the war.

This talk took place in the Weymouth Sailing Club and was

attended by Dr Ricks, who had taught me first aid for some years and was our family doctor. At the end of the evening he kindly offered me a lift back to Portland, for which I was very grateful, as the buses at that time of night were few and far between. We drew into the car-park at the beach road, and then began the most fascinating story. I had reminded him earlier in the evening of my confusion some three years before, of his being aware of my confidential appointment before I was, and I was curious to learn how this came about.

It seemed that he was one of a handful of professional people on the Island, all of whom had a certain social standing, who were, as soon as war started, co-opted into a sort of minor MI5, so that if any information at any time was required regarding a local inhabitant, then these people would be in the position to offer an opinion.

I don't know if this involvement had any official status, or if it was just that their social position made it possible to be invited to dine occasionally with the local service dignitaries.

Nonetheless, in my case Dr Ricks had been privy to confidential matters concerning me. He told me in great detail of the events during the great storm of 'D plus 19' on the beaches of Normandy, and how Admiral Swaby (flag officer in charge, Portland) had been so impressed with the report written by my commanding officer upon his return from the storm that he had promulgated a 'Special Order of the Day', something not often done. It resulted in my CO getting an accelerated second ring.

It later came to the attention of the admiral that in fact it was the CO who through weariness had wanted to beach the craft and the threat to have him court-martialled if he did, while we were seaworthy and with fuel in our tanks, had come from me, his First Lieutenant.

All this, as it happened must have been overheard down the voice-pipe to the wheelhouse below, for it was crew members who had made this known after the 'Special Order' was published.

Obviously the Admiralty now found itself in a very embarrassing position and as soon as convenient I was sent off to a command course to help correct the error.

On completion of this course I was given a senior command, of which I have written elsewhere. All these facts my local doctor had been aware of from the beginning. It also accounted for events back in Oban – why my flotilla officer had not been willing to accept a sub-lieutenant taking over what was known to be a senior command, at least not until he had phoned up the Admiralty and checked me out. Three months later I was accelerated to Lieutenant RNVR.

Number One, or 'Jimmy', for the passage out to Cochin from England was a most likeable South African named Peter Pauling. His initials were PEG, so we called him 'Peggy', which he didn't much like. He was of English stock and very young for the job – he had picked up his first ring only a short while before, having commissioned as a midshipman, or 'snotty', as they are called in the Navy. He was my choice, in place of a much older man who in my opinion had been too long aboard and who stood in the way of the many changes that I thought necessary to bring the ship up to scratch.

This change was only permitted by the FO after much heart-searching, as he had not wholeheartedly come to terms with my being in command.

'Peggy' went on to become a most willing and reliable 'Jimmy', especially when, later, we were nominated as 'arse-end charlie'.

In this capacity, plus carrying the flotilla engineering staff aboard, we had to go alongside and tow if required, until repaired, any ship that broke down during the whole of the passage out east.

This meant considerable extra work on deck for both the 'Jimmy' and the crew.

Having made the long passage across the Indian Ocean, we finally made fast in Cochin harbour, where, as we had been without mail for three weeks or so, the 'Jimmy' made for the mail office as fast as possible.

He came back with the exciting news that, being a South African, he had been officially demobbed while we were on passage – so with great haste he packed his gear and left us. In the turmoil of leaving we forgot to exchange addresses, in the ensuing years we had no contact whatever with each other.

Forty years later, my wife and I found ourselves in Johannesburgh on the first leg of a holiday that would take us first by air to Cape Town, stopping off there for five days, then by coach along the wonderful Garden Route, taking five days to get to Durban.

In Durban we broke our tour and met Phyllis Reed and family again. They were the kindly people with whom I had spent a memorable fourteen days survivors' leave forty years before. They took us northwards to the town of Merrivale, where we enjoyed their hospitality and friendship for a full week.

Rejoining the tour at Durban, we went on through the Kruger Game Park and so back to Jo'burgh.

Picking up the telephone directory, I idly thumbed through its pages – and there staring me in the face was the name P. E. G. Pauling.

I rang, but got no answer, so continued to ring every hour until bedtime. At 9.45 a man's voice answered. I asked, 'If that is P. E. G. Pauling and he can guess who this is, I'll buy him a dinner tomorrow night.'

He made a few guesses, but in the end said, 'How long ago did we last meet?' I said, 'Forty years.' A shattering 'Christ Almighty.' came over the phone. He did in the end guess correctly saying, 'Where are you phoning from?' I said, 'The Landroost Hotel.'

We had a most enjoyable dinner the next evening, having first been driven out to their ranch-style home. We talked and talked well into the night and the backlog of forty years quickly vanished. The day he left me in Cochin, in order to get a quick passage home he had volunteered for the job as 'Jimmy' in a coal-burning fleet sweeper – one of the last of the 'Smokey Joe's' – and after being demobbed he had gone to Grahamstown University and read engineering.

Back again in Jo'burgh, we lived again our past – Oban, Plymouth, Gibraltar, Malta, Port Said, the Red Sea and Aden. The kindly Paulings gave us a tour of Pretoria and then drove us to the airport and the night flight home.

Small world!

Without doubt, my most numbing experience was to have lived in such close contact with the quite endless and atrocious foul language used by the men of the fishing industry; but these rough, tough, characters were quite priceless as seamen, especially as their fishing skills could so easily be adapted to the task of mine-sweeping.

By comparison with my rather puritanical upbringing, they were callous, blasphemous and brutal, but to understand the appalling conditions in which they were forced to earn a very dubious living was to excuse the greater part of their conduct. At mealtimes, they seemed quite unable to make the simple request of 'Pass the jam, please,' without including a monstrous expletive.

They boasted, usually at breakfast-time, and in great detail, of their exploits the night before with women. I found this quite baffling, as I had been brought up in a home where I had been taught to respect other people's sisters as if they were my own, and where no profane language was ever used.

Six of the most impressionable years of my life had been spent at war, years which I would normally have spent with all the enjoyments of early manhood, a pound in my pocket, an over-indulgent mother to look after all my needs, and in my free time enjoying all the outdoor sports.

Instead, I had three years on the lower deck, living with all kinds of people and fending for myself, and advancing up the ladder to the rank of petty officer. I had been coxswain in a ship that had won commendations from the C-in-C Mediterranean for excellent seamanship.

My commanding officers in both HMS *Syringa* and HMS *Cocker* had won DSCs for the conduct of their ships in action.

These varied experiences on the lower deck were followed by three years in the wardroom – 'Gorne aft with the pigs, to be a bleeding orficer,' as they say in the messdeck.

Literally, I had come up through the hawse-pipe!

Routine and discipline I had learnt to accept. Living in unending discomfort was the norm of small ships, but I had got used to it. But the exclusive company of men over the last six years had left me uneasy and listless.

How nice it would have been now to have met again with Lieut. Commander Lawson RN and perhaps learnt from him whether his comments on my passing out for leading seaman were meant as written or had he been a brilliant psychiatrist? Perhaps he had hoped that, by damning me, he might spur me on to greater effort. Now I shall never know . . .

There is only one cure for seasickness – find a bloody great tree and go and sit under it.

Glossary
of terms not explained in the text

ETA	Estimated Time of Arrival
Jack	Union Jack; any sailor wearing bell-bottomed trousers
Lee shore	The shore facing the lee side of a ship – a dangerous place to be
Opdurating pad	On old guns it prevented the escape of gas at the rear
Trot buoy	A buoy large enough for several vessels to moor to
Watch and quarter bills	Organisational charts showing each member of the ship's company his responsibilities in any given situation
nutty	Any kind of chocolate bar.
OOW	Officer of the watch